Mexican

Delicious Mexican Recipes for Amazing Mexican Cooking

By
BookSumo Press

Published by
http://www.booksumo.com

LEGAL NOTES

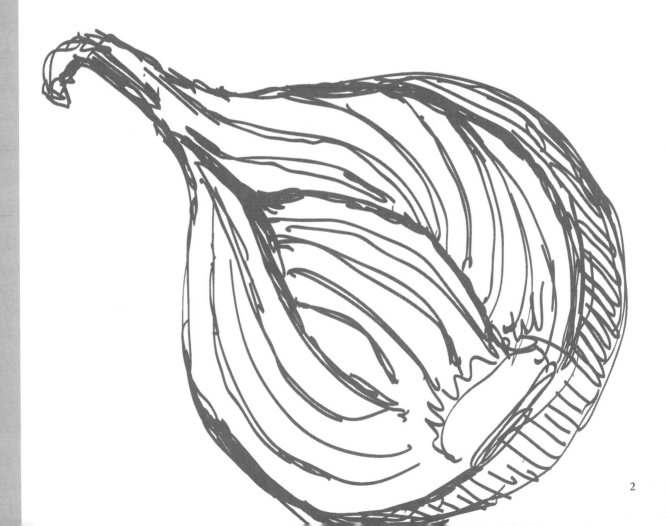

Table of Contents

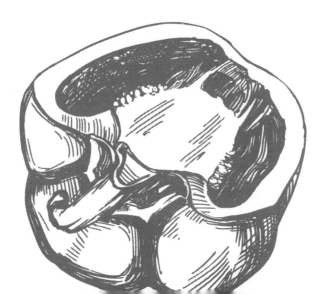

Fajita
Burgers

🥣 Prep Time: 15 mins
🕐 Total Time: 25 mins

Servings per Recipe: 4
Calories	351.0
Fat	12.8g
Cholesterol	78.3mg
Sodium	520.1mg
Carbohydrates	30.8g
Protein	29.1g

Ingredients

1/4 C. tomatillo salsa
2 tbsp avocados, chopped
1 tbsp fresh cilantro, chopped
2 slices white bread
1/2 C. onion, finely choptped
1/2 C. red bell pepper, finely chopped
1/2 C. green bell pepper, finely chopped

2 tsp fajita seasoning mix, divided
1/4 tsp salt, divided
1 tbsp tomato paste
1 lb ground turkey
1 egg white
4 whole wheat hamburger buns, toasted

Directions

1. In a small bowl, mix together the tomatillo salsa, avocado and cilantro and keep aside.
2. In a food processor, place the bread slices and pulse till a coarse crumb forms measure 1 C
3. Grease a large nonstick skillet with the nonstick spray and heat on medium-high heat.
4. Add the onion and bell peppers and sauté for about 5 minutes.
5. Stir in 1/2 tsp of the fajita seasoning and 1/8 tsp of the salt.
6. Remove from the heat and keep aside to cool.
7. In a large bowl, add 1 C. of the breadcrumbs, onion mixture, remaining 1 1/2 tsp of the fajita seasoning, remaining 1/8 tsp of the salt, tomato paste, turkey and egg white and mix till well combined.
8. With damp hands, divide the turkey mixture into 4 (3/4-inch thick) patties.
9. Grease the same skillet with the nonstick spray and heat on medium heat.
10. Add patties and cook for about 4 minutes per side.
11. Place 1 patty on bottom half of each bun and top with 1 1/2 tbsp of the salsa mixture.
12. Cover with the remaining half of the bun.

SPICY MEXICAN
Quinoa

Prep Time: 20 mins
Total Time: 40 mins

Servings per Recipe: 4
Calories	244 kcal
Fat	6.1 g
Carbohydrates	38.1g
Protein	8.1 g
Cholesterol	2 mg
Sodium	986 mg

Ingredients
1 tbsp olive oil
1 C. quinoa, rinsed
1 small onion, chopped
2 cloves garlic, minced
1 jalapeno pepper, seeded and chopped
1 (10 oz.) can diced tomatoes with green

chili peppers
1 envelope taco seasoning mix
2 C. low-sodium chicken broth
1/4 C. chopped fresh cilantro

Directions
1. In a large skillet, heat the oil on medium heat and stir fry the quinoa and onion for about 5 minutes.
2. Add the garlic and jalapeño pepper and cook for about 1-2 minutes.
3. Stir in the undrained can of diced tomatoes with green chilis, taco seasoning mix and chicken broth and bring to a boil.
4. Reduce the heat to medium-low and simmer for about 15-20 minutes.
5. Stir in cilantro and serve.

South of the Border
Pesto

🥣 Prep Time: 10 mins
🕐 Total Time: 10 mins

Servings per Recipe: 6
Calories   176 kcal
Fat   17.8 g
Cholesterol   2.4g
Sodium   2.9 g
Carbohydrates   6 mg
Protein   262 mg

Ingredients

1/4 C. hulled pumpkin seeds (pepitas)
1 bunch cilantro
1/4 C. grated cotija cheese
4 cloves garlic

1 serrano chili pepper, seeded
1/2 tsp salt
6 tbsp olive oil

Directions

1. In a food processor, add the pumpkin seeds and pulse till chopped roughly.
2. Add the remaining ingredients and pulse till smooth.

EL POLLO
Soup

🍲 Prep Time: 20 mins
🕐 Total Time: 1 h 5 mins

Servings per Recipe: 4
Calories	335 kcal
Fat	7.7 g
Carbohydrates	37.7g
Protein	31.5 g
Cholesterol	62 mg
Sodium	841 mg

Ingredients

3 cooked, boneless chicken breast halves, shredded
1 (15 oz.) can kidney beans
1 C. whole kernel corn
1 (14.5 oz.) can stewed tomatoes
1/2 C. chopped onion

1/2 green bell pepper, chopped
1/2 red bell pepper, chopped
1 (4 oz.) can chopped green chili peppers
2 (14.5 oz.) cans chicken broth
1 tbsp ground cumin

Directions

1. In a large pan mix together all the ingredients on medium heat.

2. Simmer for about 45 minutes.

Restaurant-Style
Latin Rice

Prep Time: 20 mins
Total Time: 55 mins

Servings per Recipe: 6

Calories	510 kcal
Fat	18.3 g
Carbohydrates	59.1g
Protein	28.3 g
Cholesterol	74 mg
Sodium	1294 mg

Ingredients

1 lb. lean ground beef
1 onion, diced
1 green bell pepper, diced
1 (14 oz.) can beef broth
2 C. fresh corn kernels
1 (10 oz.) can diced tomatoes with green chili peppers
1 (15 oz.) can tomato sauce
1/2 C. salsa

1/2 tsp chili powder
1/2 tsp paprika
1/2 tsp garlic powder
1/2 tsp salt
1/2 tsp ground black pepper
1 tsp minced cilantro
1 1/2 C. uncooked white rice
1 C. shredded Cheddar cheese

Directions

1. Heat a medium pan on medium heat and cook the beef till browned completely.
2. Drain off the grease from the pan.
3. Add the onion and green pepper and cook till the onion becomes tender.
4. Stir in the beef broth, corn, tomatoes with green chili peppers and tomato sauce, salsa, chili powder, paprika, garlic powder, salt, pepper and cilantro and bring to a boil.
5. Stir in the rice and cook, covered for about 25 minutes.
6. Top with the Cheddar cheese and cook for about 10 minutes.

CANELA
Brownies

Prep Time: 20 mins
Total Time: 1 h 10 mins

Servings per Recipe: 30
Calories   206 kcal
Fat   10.8 g
Carbohydrates   27g
Protein   2.7 g
Cholesterol   62 mg
Sodium   76 mg

Ingredients

1 1/2 C. unsalted butter
3 C. white sugar
6 eggs
1 tbsp vanilla extract
1 1/4 C. unsweetened cocoa powder
1 1/2 C. all-purpose flour

1 3/4 tsp ground Mexican cinnamon (canela)
1/2 tsp ground pequin chili pepper
3/4 tsp kosher salt
3/4 tsp baking powder

Directions

1. Set your oven to 350 degrees F before doing anything else and line a 15x12-inch baking dish with the parchment paper, leaving about 3 inches of paper overhanging 2 sides to use as handles.
2. In a microwave-safe bowl, add the butter and microwave on Medium for about 1 minute.
3. Add the sugar and mix till well combined.
4. Add the eggs, one at a time, and mix till well combined.
5. Stir in the vanilla extract.
6. In a bowl, sift together the flour, cocoa, cinnamon, pequin pepper, salt and baking powder.
7. Add the flour mixture into the butter mixture and mix till well combined.
8. Transfer the mixture into the prepared baking dish evenly.
9. Cook in the oven for about 20-25 minutes or till a toothpick inserted into the center comes out clean.
10. Remove from the oven and keep aside to cool in the pan.
11. Remove the parchment paper handles to remove the brownies for slicing.

Ground Beef
Mexican Dip

Prep Time: 25 mins
Total Time: 50 mins

Servings per Recipe: 32
Calories	150 kcal
Fat	11.3 g
Carbohydrates	3.9g
Protein	8.3 g
Cholesterol	30 mg
Sodium	429 mg

Ingredients
1 lb. ground beef
1 (16 oz.) jar salsa
1 (10.75 oz.) can condensed cream of
mushroom soup
2 lb. processed cheese food, cubed

Directions
1. Heat a medium pan on medium-high heat and cook the beef till browned completely.
2. Drain off the grease from the pan.
3. In a slow cooker, transfer the cooked beef with the salsa, condensed cream of mushroom soup and processed cheese food.
4. Set the slow cooker on High till cheese melts completely.
5. Now, set the slow cooker on Low and simmer till serving.

PEPPERJACK
Pizza

Prep Time: 20 mins
Total Time: 32 mins

Servings per Recipe: 6
Calories	373 kcal
Fat	15.3 g
Carbohydrates	44g
Protein	17 g
Cholesterol	26 mg
Sodium	1027 mg

Ingredients

1/2 (16 oz.) can spicy fat-free refried beans
1 C. salsa, divided
1 (12 inch) pre-baked Italian pizza crust
2 C. shredded hearts of romaine lettuce
3 medium green onions, thinly sliced
1/4 C. ranch dressing

1/4 C. crumbled tortilla chips
1 C. shredded pepper Jack cheese

Directions

1. Set your oven to 450 degrees F before doing anything else and arrange a rack in the lowest portion of the oven.
2. In a bowl, mix together the beans and 1/2 C. of the salsa.
3. Arrange the crust on a cookie sheet and top with the bean mixture evenly.
4. Cook in the oven for about 10 minutes.
5. Remove from the oven and place the lettuce, green onions over the beans mixture.
6. Top with the remaining salsa.
7. Drizzle with the dressing evenly and top with the chips and cheese evenly.
8. Cook in the oven for about 2 minutes more.
9. Cut into 6 slices and serve.

Quick Midweek
Mexican Macaroni

Prep Time: 20 mins
Total Time: 50 mins

Servings per Recipe: 8

Calories	374 kcal
Fat	21.4 g
Carbohydrates	23.5g
Protein	22.9 g
Cholesterol	79 mg
Sodium	997 mg

Ingredients
1 C. dry macaroni
1 lb. ground beef
1 small onion, chopped
1 (11 oz.) can whole kernel corn, drained

1 (10 oz.) can diced tomatoes with green chili peppers, drained
1 (1 lb.) loaf processed cheese, cubed

Directions
1. In large pan of the boiling water, add the macaroni for about 8 minutes.
2. Drain well.
3. Meanwhile, heat a medium skillet on medium-high heat and cook the beef till browned completely.
4. Add the onion and cook till browned.
5. Drain off the grease from the skillet.
6. Reduce the heat to medium and stir in the corn, tomatoes, cheese and cooked noodles.
7. Cook, stirring gently till bubbly.

CANCUN STYLE
Caviar

🥣 Prep Time: 10 mins

🕐 Total Time: 6 h 10 mins

Servings per Recipe: 32

Calories	17 kcal
Fat	1.5 g
Cholesterol	0.9g
Sodium	0.2 g
Carbohydrates	0 mg
Protein	188 mg

Ingredients

2 large tomatoes, finely chopped
5 green onions, chopped
3 tbsp olive oil
3 1/2 tbsp tarragon vinegar
1 (4 oz.) can chopped green chili peppers

1 (2.25 oz.) can chopped black olives
1 tsp garlic salt
1 tsp salt

Directions

1. In a medium bowl, mix together all the ingredients.

2. Refrigerate, covered for about 6 hours or overnight before serving.

Puerto Vallarta
Eggplant

Prep Time: 10 mins
Total Time: 25 mins

Servings per Recipe: 4
Calories	349 kcal
Fat	23.3 g
Carbohydrates	6.8g
Protein	27.4 g
Cholesterol	101 mg
Sodium	542 mg

Ingredients

1 lb. ground beef
1/4 C. chopped onion
1 tbsp all-purpose flour
1 (8 oz.) can tomato sauce
1/4 C. chopped green bell pepper
1 tsp dried oregano

1 tsp chili powder
1 eggplant, cut into 1/2-inch slices
salt and ground black pepper to taste
1 C. shredded Cheddar cheese

Directions

1. Heat a large skillet on medium-high heat and cook the ground beef and onion for about 5-7 minutes.
2. Drain the grease from the skillet.
3. Sprinkle the flour over the beef mixture and toss to coat.
4. Stir in the tomato sauce, green bell pepper, oregano and chili powder.
5. Sprinkle the eggplant slices with the salt and pepper and place over the beef mixture.
6. Simmer, covered for about 10-15 minutes.
7. Serve with a topping of the Cheddar cheese.

SLOW COOKER
Nachos

🍳 Prep Time: 20 mins
🕐 Total Time: 4 h 20 mins

Servings per Recipe: 15
Calories	241.5
Fat	16.2g
Cholesterol	67.4mg
Sodium	1067.5mg
Carbohydrates	7.6g
Protein	16.1g

Ingredients

1 lb. lean ground beef
2 - 3 cloves garlic, minced
2 (16 oz.) packages Velveeta Mexican cheese, cut into cubes
2 (10 oz.) cans Rotel Tomatoes, drained

1/2 C. chopped green onion
tortilla chips

Directions

1. Heat a large skillet and cook the beef and garlic until it is browned completely.
2. Drain the fat from the skillet.
3. Transfer the beef mixture in a large slow cooker with the tomatoes and cheese and stir to combine.
4. Set the slow cooker on Low and cook, covered for about 3-4 hours, stirring once after 2 hours.
5. Uncover and stir in the onions.
6. Serve the beef mixture with the tortilla chips.

Licuado
de Mango

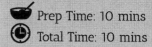 Prep Time: 10 mins

Total Time: 10 mins

Servings per Recipe: 2

Calories	255 kcal
Carbohydrates	52.1 g
Cholesterol	15 mg
Fat	3.9 g
Protein	6.7 g
Sodium	82 mg

Ingredients

1 mango, peeled, seeded and diced
1 1/2 cups milk

3 tbsps honey
1 cup ice cubes

Directions

1. Blend all the ingredients mentioned above until the required smoothness is achieved.
2. Serve

MEXICAN
Veggie Puree

Prep Time: 25 mins
Total Time: 35 mins

Servings per Recipe: 4
Calories	167 kcal
Fat	14.1 g
Carbohydrates	8.3g
Protein	4.1 g
Cholesterol	0 mg
Sodium	363 mg

Ingredients

6 spears fresh asparagus, trimmed and cut into 1/2 inch pieces
1 C. bite-size cauliflower florets
2 stalks celery ribs, chopped
1/3 C. canned kidney beans, drained
1/3 C. chopped hazelnuts
2/3 tsp chopped fresh dill
1/4 tsp dried basil

1/2 tsp minced garlic
2 tbsp sunflower seed oil
1/3 tsp chili powder
1/4 tsp celery seed
1/2 tsp salt

Directions

1. Steam the asparagus and cauliflower for about 10 minutes.
2. Transfer the vegetables into a bowl and stir in the celery.
3. In a blender, add the kidney beans, hazelnuts, dill, basil, garlic, oil, chili powder, celery seed and salt and pulse till smooth.
4. Pour the sauce over the vegetables mixture and serve.

Classical
Mexican Ceviche

Prep Time: 30 mins
Total Time: 120 mins

Servings per Recipe: 8
Calories	387 kcal
Fat	12.4 g
Carbohydrates	57.6g
Protein	17.7 g
Cholesterol	86 mg
Sodium	733 mg

Ingredients
5 large lemons, juiced
1 lb. jumbo shrimp, peeled and deveined
1/4 C. chopped fresh cilantro
tomato and clam juice cocktail
2 white onions, finely chopped
1 cucumber, peeled and finely chopped

1 large tomatoes, seeded and chopped
3 fresh jalapeno peppers, seeded and minced
1 bunch radishes, finely diced
2 cloves fresh garlic, minced
tortilla chips

Directions
1. In a bowl, add the shrimp and enough lemon juice to cover the shrimp completely.
2. Refrigerate, covered for about 30 minutes.
3. Remove the bowl of shrimp from the refrigerator.
4. Add the tomatoes, onions, cucumber, radishes and garlic and toss to coat.
5. Slowly, stir in the cilantro and jalapeño peppers.
6. Stir in the tomato and clam juice and refrigerate, covered for about 1 hour.
7. Serve chilled with the tortilla chips.

HONEY & BEANS
Latin Salad

Prep Time: 20 mins
Total Time: 40 mins

Servings per Recipe: 6
Calories	10.6 g
Fat	34.8g
Cholesterol	8.2 g
Sodium	0 mg
Carbohydrates	358 mg
Protein	10.6 g

Ingredients

1 (15 oz.) can black beans, rinsed and drained
1 (15 oz.) can garbanzo beans, drained
2 C. frozen corn kernels
1/2 onion, finely diced
1 tbsp chopped fresh cilantro
2 jalapeno peppers, seeded and minced (optional)

1 red bell pepper, diced
1/4 C. olive oil
3 tbsp fresh lime juice
1 tsp ground black pepper
salt to taste
1/2 tsp honey

Directions

1. In a large bowl, add all the ingredients and mix well.

2. Refrigerate till the flavors blends completely.

Taco Tuesday's
Lasagna

Prep Time: 25 mins
Total Time: 45 mins

Servings per Recipe: 5	
Calories	447 kcal
Fat	24 g
Carbohydrates	33.2g
Protein	23.2 g
Cholesterol	79 mg
Sodium	899 mg

Ingredients

1 lb. lean ground beef
1 (1 oz.) package taco seasoning mix
1 (14 oz.) can peeled and diced tomatoes with juice
10 (6 inch) corn tortillas

1 C. prepared salsa
1/2 C. shredded Colby cheese

Directions

1. Set your oven to 350 degrees F before doing anything else.
2. Heat a large skillet on medium-high heat and cook the beef till browned completely.
3. Stir in the taco seasoning and tomatoes.
4. In the bottom of a 13x9-inch baking dish, arrange half of the tortillas evenly.
5. Place the beef mixture over the tortillas evenly.
6. Place the remaining tortillas over the beef mixture and top with the salsa, followed by the cheese.
7. Cook in the oven for about 20-30 minutes.

A MEXICAN
Corn Drink for Winter

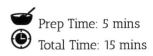
Prep Time: 5 mins
Total Time: 15 mins

Servings per Recipe: 5
Calories	68 kcal
Fat	0.4 g
Carbohydrates	14.1g
Protein	1.1 g
Cholesterol	0 mg
Sodium	8 mg

Ingredients
1/2 C. masa (corn flour)
5 C. water
1 tbsp ground cinnamon

5 tbsp piloncillo, brown sugar cones
1 tbsp vanilla extract

Directions
1. In a blender, add the masa, water, cinnamon and piloncillo and pulse till smooth.
2. Transfer the mixture into a pan and bring to a boil on medium heat, stirring continuously.
3. Reduce the heat to low and simmer, stirring continuously for about 5 minutes.
4. Remove from the heat and stir in the vanilla.
5. Place into the mugs and serve hot.

A Baked
Mexican Medley

Prep Time: 5 mins
Total Time: 1 hr 5 mins

Servings per Recipe: 8
Calories   480 kcal
Fat   26.6 g
Carbohydrates   24g
Protein   34.8 g
Cholesterol   104 mg
Sodium   1103 mg

Ingredients

1 (10.75 oz.) can condensed cream of mushroom soup
1 (10.75 oz.) can condensed cream of chicken soup
1 (4 oz.) can chopped green chili peppers, drained
1/4 C. milk

2/3 C. sour cream
8 (6 inch) flour tortillas
6 boneless chicken breast halves, cooked and cubed
2 C. shredded Cheddar cheese

Directions

1. Set your oven to 350 degrees F before doing anything else and lightly, grease a 13x9-inch baking dish.
2. In a medium bowl, add the cream of mushroom soup, cream of chicken soup, chili peppers, milk and sour cream and mix till well combined.
3. In the bottom of the prepared baking dish, arrange a layer of the tortilla strips.
4. Place 1/2 of the soup mixture, followed by 1/2 of the chicken and 1/2 of the shredded cheese.
5. Repeat the layers till all the ingredients are used completely, ending with a layer of the shredded cheese.
6. Cook, covered in the oven for about 45 minutes.
7. Uncover and cook for about 15 minutes more.

PEPPERJACK
Spicy Wontons

Prep Time: 10 mins
Total Time: 20 mins

Servings per Recipe: 13
Calories	240 kcal
Fat	13.4 g
Carbohydrates	18.7g
Protein	10.4 g
Cholesterol	40 mg
Sodium	385 mg

Ingredients
1 lb. pepper-jack cheese, finely shredded
1 (14 oz.) package won ton wrappers
1 C. vegetable oil for deep frying

Directions
1. In the center of each wonton skin, place 1-2 tsp of the shredded cheese.
2. Fold the top and bottom corners toward each other and roll it up like a little egg roll.
3. With wet fingers, seal the wonton.
4. In a deep pan, heat the oil to 365 degrees F and fry the wontons in batches.
5. Drain on paper towels.
6. Serve immediately.

Guacamole 101

Prep Time: 10 mins
Total Time: 10 mins

Servings per Recipe: 3

Calories	371 kcal
Fat	29.8 g
Cholesterol	28.9g
Sodium	5.7 g
Carbohydrates	0 mg
Protein	22 mg

Ingredients

3 avocados, peeled and mashed
1 red onion, minced
1 red bell pepper, chopped
1/2 yellow bell pepper, chopped

1 green bell pepper, chopped
1 fresh jalapeno pepper, chopped
1/3 C. chopped fresh cilantro
1 lime, juiced

Directions

1. In a large bowl, add all the ingredients and mix well.
2. Refrigerate, covered before serving.

REFRIED
Meatloaf

Prep Time: 25 mins
Total Time: 70 mins

Servings per Recipe: 8	
Calories	488 kcal
Fat	28.8 g
Carbohydrates	27g
Protein	27.8 g
Cholesterol	99 mg
Sodium	886 mg

Ingredients

2 lb. lean ground beef
1 (1.25 oz.) package taco seasoning mix
1 (16 oz.) can refried beans
4 (8 inch) flour tortillas

3/4 C. fresh salsa
1/2 C. shredded Cheddar cheese

Directions

1. Set your oven to 350 degrees F before doing anything else.
2. In a medium bowl, add the ground beef and taco seasoning and mix well.
3. In a medium pan, add the refried beans on medium-low and cook till heated completely.
4. Place the ground beef mixture over a large foil paper and press into an about 1-inch thick square shape.
5. Place the refried beans over the flattened beef evenly.
6. Top with the flour tortillas, trimming the edges to fit the square.
7. Top with the salsa and Cheddar cheese, keeping 1/2-1 inch away from the edges of the square.
8. Gently roll the layered beef into a Swiss roll shape, pressing the loaf.
9. Pinch and seal the edges.
10. Wrap in the foil paper and seal.
11. Cook in the oven for about 40-45 minutes.
12. Cut the loaf in half to test the doneness.

Mexican
Tostadas

Prep Time: 10 mins
Total Time: 35 mins

Servings per Recipe: 8	
Calories	402 kcal
Fat	20 g
Carbohydrates	20.5g
Protein	33.6 g
Cholesterol	91 mg
Sodium	395 mg

Ingredients
2 tbsp olive oil
1 large onion, cut into rings
1 (15 oz.) can stewed tomatoes
1 (7 oz.) can chipotle peppers in adobo
sauce
2 lb. shredded cooked chicken meat
16 tostada shells
1/2 C. sour cream

Directions
1. In a pan, heat the oil on medium heat and sauté the onions for about 5 minutes.
2. Meanwhile, in a blender, add the tomatoes, chipotle peppers and adobo sauce and pulse till pureed.
3. Transfer the tomato mixture into the pan with the chicken.
4. Simmer, covered for about 20 minutes.
5. Place the chicken mixture onto tostada shells and top with a dollop of the sour cream.

GUADALAJARA
Gravy

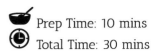 Prep Time: 10 mins
Total Time: 30 mins

Servings per Recipe: 6
Calories	170 kcal
Fat	14.2 g
Carbohydrates	10.1g
Protein	1.5 g
Cholesterol	0 mg
Sodium	420 mg

Ingredients
1/2 C. flour
2 tbsp chili powder
2 tsp onion powder
1 tsp dried Mexican oregano

1 tsp salt
6 tbsp vegetable oil
4 C. water

Directions
1. In a bowl, mix together the flour, chili powder, onion powder, oregano and salt.
2. In a large pan, heat the oil on low heat.
3. Slowly, add the flour mixture, beating continuously till smooth.
4. Slowly, add the water, beating continuously till smooth and bring to a gentle simmer.
5. Simmer for about 5 minutes.
6. Remove from the heat and cool for about 10 minutes.

San Luis
Salmon

Prep Time: 20 mins
Total Time: 1 h 30 mins

Servings per Recipe: 4
Calories	394 kcal
Fat	21.6 g
Carbohydrates	11.9g
Protein	38.2 g
Cholesterol	119 mg
Sodium	298 mg

Ingredients

2 tbsp olive oil
2 limes, juiced
2 marinated roasted red peppers, with liquid
1 clove garlic, finely chopped
1/8 tsp ground allspice
1/8 tsp ground cinnamon
1/4 tsp ground cumin
1/4 tsp white sugar

salt and pepper to taste
1 1/2 lb. salmon steaks
1 large tomato, cut into thin wedges
3 green onions, chopped
1 C. shredded lettuce
1 lime, sliced

Directions

1. In a large nonreactive bowl, mix together the olive oil, juice of the 2 limes, roasted red peppers, garlic, allspice, cinnamon, cumin, sugar, salt and pepper.
2. Add the salmon steaks and rub with the mixture evenly.
3. Refrigerate, covered for at least 1 hour.
4. Set the broiler of your oven.
5. In a broiler pan, place the salmon steaks in a single layer.
6. Cook under the broiler for about 3-5 minutes per side.
7. In a small bowl, mix together the tomato wedges and green onions.
8. Serve salmon with the tomato mixture, lettuce and lime wedges.

SPICY
Chili Mango

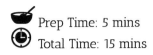
Prep Time: 5 mins
Total Time: 15 mins

Servings per Recipe: 2
Calories	85 kcal
Fat	0.9 g
Carbohydrates	21.7g
Protein	1.1 g
Cholesterol	0 mg
Sodium	237 mg

Ingredients
1/4 C. water
1 tbsp chili powder
1 pinch salt
3 tbsp lemon juice
1 mango - peeled, seeded, and sliced

Directions
1. In a pan, add the water and bring to a boil.
2. Add the chili powder, salt and lemon juice and mix till smooth and hot.
3. Add the sliced mango and toss to coat.
4. Keep aside for a few minutes before serving.

Shredded
Turkey for Tacos

Prep Time: 10 mins
Total Time: 25 mins

Servings per Recipe: 4
Calories	225 kcal
Fat	6.9 g
Carbohydrates	4.9 g
Protein	34.1 g
Cholesterol	86 mg
Sodium	180 mg

Ingredients

1 tsp vegetable oil
1 onion, chopped
1 lb. shredded cooked turkey
1 tsp garlic powder

1 large fresh tomato, chopped
1/2 C. water
1 tbsp chopped fresh cilantro
salt and pepper to taste

Directions

1. In a skillet, heat the oil on medium heat and sauté the onion till tender.
2. Add the turkey, garlic powder, tomato, water, cilantro, salt and pepper.
3. Simmer, covered for about 5 minutes.

MEXICAN MONDAY'S
Elbow Macaroni Dinner

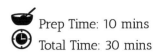

Prep Time: 10 mins

Total Time: 30 mins

Servings per Recipe: 6

Calories	588 kcal
Fat	20.4 g
Carbohydrates	70.6g
Protein	32.3 g
Cholesterol	76 mg
Sodium	1258 mg

Ingredients
1 lb. ground beef
1/2 onion, chopped
1 (12 oz.) package elbow macaroni
1/2 lb. processed cheese (such as Velveeta(R)), diced

1 1/2 C. salsa
1 (15 oz.) can pinto beans, drained and rinsed
1 (14 oz.) can whole kernel corn, drained

Directions
1. Heat a large skillet on medium heat and cook the beef and onion for about 10 minutes.
2. Drain the excess grease from the skillet.
3. Meanwhile in large pan of the lightly salted boiling water, cook the macaroni for about 8 minutes.
4. Drain well.
5. Add the macaroni in the pan with the beef mixture on medium-low heat.
6. Stir in the processed cheese for about 3 minutes.
7. Stir in the salsa, pinto beans and corn and cook for about 5 minutes.

South-American
Sushi

Prep Time: 20 mins
Total Time: 50 mins

Servings per Recipe: 6
Calories   332 kcal
Fat   15.6 g
Cholesterol   40.5g
Sodium   9.3 g
Carbohydrates   11 mg
Protein   708 mg

Ingredients

3 oz. low-fat cream cheese, softened
1 1/2 tbsp seeded and finely chopped
chipotle in adobo
1 large plain flour tortilla
1 large tomato-flavored tortilla
1 large spinach-flavored tortilla

3/4 C. low-fat refried black beans
6 tbsp pico de gallo salsa
1 1/2 Avocados from Mexico, peeled, pitted
and diced
3/4 C. chopped cilantro leaves

Directions

1. In a bowl, mix together the cream cheese and chipotle.
2. Heat the tortillas in microwave to soften.
3. Spread about 2 tbsp of the chipotle cream cheese, 1/4 C. of black beans and 2 tbsp of the salsa over each tortilla.
4. Top with 1/3 of the avocado and cilantro.
5. Roll up the tortillas tightly.
6. With a plastic wrap, wrap the each tortilla and refrigerate.
7. Just before the serving, trim the ends.
8. Cut each roll across into 6 pieces.

A MEXICAN
Pasta

Prep Time: 5 mins
Total Time: 25 mins

Servings per Recipe: 8
Calories	439 kcal
Fat	16.6 g
Carbohydrates	49.2g
Protein	24.2 g
Cholesterol	60 mg
Sodium	890 mg

Ingredients
1 (16 oz.) package mostaccioli pasta
1 lb. ground beef
1 (24 oz.) jar picante sauce

1 (15 oz.) can stewed tomatoes with juice
1 1/2 C. shredded Mexican-style cheese

Directions
1. In large pan of the lightly salted boiling water, cook the mostaccioli for about 11 minutes.
2. Drain well.
3. Heat a large skillet on medium-high heat and cook the beef and onion for about 5-7 minutes.
4. Drain any excess grease.
5. Add the picante sauce and stewed tomatoes and cook for about 10 minutes, stirring occasionally.
6. Gently stir the cooked mostaccioli into the ground beef mixture.
7. Add Mexican-style cheese and cook for about 5 minutes.

Caribbean x Mexican
Chuck Roast

Prep Time: 30 mins
Total Time: 16 h 40 mins

Servings per Recipe: 24
Calories	175 kcal
Fat	12.5 g
Carbohydrates	1.2g
Protein	13.5 g
Cholesterol	52 mg
Sodium	34 mg

Ingredients
4 dried guajillo chilies
2 tsp cumin seeds
1/8 whole cloves
1 C. boiling water
1/2 tsp ground ancho chili powder
1 large onion, quartered
6 cloves garlic

2 tsp dried oregano
1 tsp ground thyme
1/3 C. apple cider vinegar
2 tsp lime juice
1 (6 lb.) boneless beef chuck roast
2 bay leaves

Directions
1. Heat a heavy skillet on medium heat and cook the dried guajillo chilis for about 5 minutes, turning occasionally.
2. Remove from the heat and keep aside to cool for a moment.
3. Meanwhile in a hot skillet, toast the cumin and cloves.
4. Remove from the pan and keep aside.
5. Remove and discard the stems, seeds and veins of the chilis and place into a small bowl.
6. Place the boiling water over top and keep aside, covered for about 1 hour.
7. Grind the toasted cumin and cloves into a powder form.
8. Remove the chilis from the soaking water, and place into the blender along with 1/3 C. of the soaking liquid, ancho chili powder, onion, garlic, oregano, thyme, vinegar, lime juice, powdered cumin and cloves and pulse till a smooth paste forms.
9. In a bowl, add the guajillo chili paste.
10. Add the beef roast and coat with the paste evenly. With a plastic wrap, cover the bowl and refrigerate to marinate for overnight.
11. Set your oven to 325 degrees F.
12. In a roasting pan, place the roast and marinade and top with the bay leaves.
13. With a foil paper, cover tightly and cook in the oven for about 6 hours.
14. Remove from the oven and keep aside, covered at the room temperature for about 1 hour.
15. Discard the bay leaves and shred with two forks before serving

REAL
Authentic Tamales

Prep Time: 5 h 30 m
Total Time: 6 h 30 m

Servings per Recipe: 36
Calories	347 kcal
Fat	24.4 g
Carbohydrates	23.3g
Protein	9.1 g
Cholesterol	38 mg
Sodium	248 mg

Ingredients

4 lb. boneless chuck roast
4 cloves garlic
3 (8 oz.) packages dried corn husks
4 dried ancho chilis
2 tbsp vegetable oil
2 tbsp all-purpose flour
1 C. beef broth
1 tsp cumin seeds
1 tsp ground cumin

2 cloves garlic, minced
2 tsp chopped fresh oregano
1 tsp red pepper flakes
1 tsp white vinegar
salt to taste
3 C. lard
1 tbsp salt
9 C. masa harina

Directions

1. In a large pan, add the beef, garlic and enough cold water to cover on high heat and bring to a boil.
2. Reduce the heat and simmer, covered for about 3 1/2 hours.
3. Remove the beef from the pan and keep aside to cool, then shred it.
4. Reserve 5 C. of the cooking liquid and discard the garlic.
5. Meanwhile, in a large container, place the corn husks and cover with the warm water.
6. Place an inverted plate and a heavy can to weight down and keep aside for about 3 hours.
7. In a cast iron skillet, toast the ancho chilis.
8. Keep aside to cool and then remove the stems and seeds.
9. Crumble and grind in a clean coffee grinder.
10. In a large skillet, heat the oil.
11. Add the flour and cook, stirring till browned slightly.
12. Add about 1 C. of the beef broth and stir till smooth.
13. Add the shredded beef, ground chilis, cumin seeds, ground cumin, minced garlic, oregano, red pepper flakes, vinegar and salt.

14. Simmer, covered for about 45 minutes.
15. In a large bowl, add the lard and salt and with an electric mixer, beat on high speed till fluffy.
16. Add the masa harina and beat at low speed till well combined.
17. Slowly, add the reserved cooking liquid and beating contiguously till mixture becomes like a soft cookie dough.
18. Drain water from the corn husks.
19. One at a time, flatten out each husk, with the narrow end facing you.
20. Spread about 2 tbsp of the masa mixture onto the top 2/3 of the husk.
21. Spread about 1 tbsp of meat mixture down the middle of the masa.
22. Roll up the corn husk starting at one of the long sides.
23. Fold the narrow end of the husk onto the rolled tamale and tie with a piece of butchers' twine.
24. In a steamer basket, place the tamales and steam over boiling water for about 1 hour.
25. Serve immediately.

MAIZE
Flour Drink

Prep Time: 5 m
Total Time: 35 m

Servings per Recipe: 12
Calories	524 kcal
Fat	3.9 g
Carbohydrates	63.3g
Protein	3.4 g
Cholesterol	7 mg
Sodium	276 mg

Ingredients
1 1/2 C. water
1 cinnamon stick
1 whole clove
1 pod star anise
4 1/4 C. milk
2 tablets Mexican chocolate

3/4 C. pinole (coarse ground maize flour)
1 pinch crushed piloncillo (Mexican brown sugar cone)

Directions
1. In a pan, add the water, cinnamon stick, clove and star anise and bring to a boil.
2. Remove from the heat and keep aside, covered for about 10 minutes.
3. Strain the spice water.
4. In another pan, heat the milk, chocolate, and pinole on medium heat, beating continuously for about 10 minutes.
5. Remove from the heat and add the piloncillo and keep aside for about 5 minutes more.
6. Add the spice water into the chocolate mixture and stir to combine.

Back-To-School
Fajitas

🥄 Prep Time: 15 mins
🕐 Total Time: 35 mins

Servings per Recipe: 4
Calories	223.7
Fat	11.8g
Cholesterol	43.7mg
Sodium	244.5mg
Carbohydrates	4.1g
Protein	24.1g

Ingredients

12 oz. boneless skinless chicken breasts
4 (8 inch) spinach tortillas
1 tbsp cooking oil
1/3 C. finely chopped onion
1/3 C. finely chopped green sweet pepper
1/2 C. chopped tomato
2 tbsp bottled reduced-fat Italian salad

dressing
1/2 C. shredded reduced-fat cheddar cheese
1/4 C. bottled salsa
1/4 C. light sour cream (optional)

Directions

1. Set your oven to 350 degrees F before doing anything else.
2. Cut the chicken into bite-size strips.
3. Wrap the tortillas in aluminum foil and heat in the oven.
4. In a 12-inch skillet, heat the oil on medium-high heat.
5. Add the chicken, onion and green pepper and cook for about 2-3 minutes.
6. Remove from heat. Drain well.
7. Stir in the tomato and salad dressing.
8. Fill the warm tortillas with the beef mixture and roll up tortillas.
9. Serve with cheese, salsa and sour cream.

PORTOBELLO
Onion Pepper Fajitas

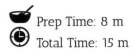

Prep Time: 8 m
Total Time: 15 m

Servings per Recipe: 4
Calories	255.6
Fat	7.3g
Cholesterol	0.0mg
Sodium	405.4mg
Carbohydrates	40.7g
Protein	8.2g

Ingredients
2 tsp oil
4 large portabella mushrooms, stems removed
2 medium bell peppers, sliced
1 medium onion, sliced
1 (1 1/8 oz.) packets fajita seasoning mix
1 tbsp balsamic vinegar (optional)

8 lettuce leaves
8 soft taco-size flour tortillas, warmed
sour cream
fresh cilantro stem

Directions
1. Heat 1 tsp of the oil in each of 2 skillets on medium-high heat.
2. In 1 skillet, add the mushrooms and cook for about 4 minutes, stirring occasionally.
3. Stir in the balsamic vinegar and cook for about 2 minutes.
4. In another skillet, add the peppers and cook for about 6 minutes, stirring occasionally.
5. Transfer the mushrooms onto a cutting board and slice them.
6. Stir the seasoning and 1/3 C. of the water into the pepper mixture and cook for about 1 minute.
7. Roll up with peppers and onions in lettuce-lined tortillas.
8. Serve with a garnishing of the sour cream and cilantro.

Fresh Green
Enchiladas

Prep Time: 45 mins
Total Time: 1 h 20 mins

Servings per Recipe: 4
Calories	559 kcal
Fat	25 g
Carbohydrates	48.9 g
Protein	37.1 g
Cholesterol	84 mg
Sodium	1344 mg

Ingredients

2 bone-in chicken breast halves
2 C. chicken broth
1/4 white onion
1 clove garlic
2 tsp salt
1 lb. fresh tomatillos, husks removed
5 serrano peppers
1/4 white onion

1 clove garlic
1 pinch salt
12 corn tortillas
1/4 C. vegetable oil
1 C. crumbled queso fresco
1/2 white onion, chopped
1 bunch fresh cilantro, chopped

Directions

1. In a pan, mix together the chicken breast, broth, 1/4 of the onion, 1 garlic clove and 2 tsp of the salt and bring to a boil.
2. Boil for about 20 minutes.
3. Transfer the chicken into a plate and keep aside to cool.
4. Strain the broth and reserve it.
5. Discard the onion and garlic.
6. After cooling, shred the chicken.
7. In a pan, add the tomatillos and serrano chilis with enough water to cover and bring to a boil.
8. Boil till the tomatillos turn into a dull army green color.
9. Strain the tomatillos mixture and transfer in a blender.
10. Add reserved broth, 1/4 of the onion, 1 garlic clove and a pinch of salt and pulse till pureed finely.
11. Transfer the salsa in a medium pan and bring to a gentle simmer.
12. In a frying pan, heat the oil and fry the tortillas, one by one.
13. Transfer the tortillas on a paper towel to drain.
14. Dip the slightly fried tortillas in low-boiling green salsa slightly.
15. Divide the tortillas into the serving plates.
16. Top the tortillas with the shredded chicken, followed by the extra green sauce, crumbled cheese, chopped onion and chopped cilantro.

RED, WHITE, and Green Soup

🥣 Prep Time: 30 m
🕐 Total Time: 8 h 30 m

Servings per Recipe: 8
Calories	225 kcal
Fat	5.3 g
Carbohydrates	31.8g
Protein	14.3 g
Cholesterol	139 mg
Sodium	1679 mg

Ingredients

3 gallons water, divided
2 1/2 lb. beef tripe, cut into 1-inch pieces
6 cloves garlic, finely chopped
1 large white onion, finely chopped
1 1/2 tbsp salt
1 tbsp ground black pepper
1 1/2 tbsp dried oregano
2 tbsp ground red pepper

5 de arbol chili peppers
6 japones chili peppers, seeds removed
6 C. canned white hominy, drained
1/2 white onion, chopped
1/4 C. chopped fresh cilantro
2 limes, juiced

Directions

1. In a large pan, bring 1 gallon water to a boil and add the tripe.
2. Reduce the heat and simmer for about 2 hours.
3. With a spoon, skim off the fat occasionally.
4. Drain the water and add a fresh gallon of the water.
5. Simmer for about 2 hours.
6. Drain well.
7. Add the remaining 1 gallon water in the pan with tripe and bring to a boil.
8. Stir in the garlic, 1 white onion, salt, pepper, oregano and red pepper.
9. Reduce heat and simmer for about 1 hour.
10. Set the broiler of your oven.
11. Place the de arbol chili peppers on a baking sheet and cook under the broiler for about 2 minutes.
12. Remove from the oven and slit lengthwise, then remove the seeds.
13. In a food processor, add the de arbol chili peppers and japones chili peppers and pulse till chopped finely.
14. Add the pepper mixture into the pan and cook for about 2 hours on low heat.
15. Stir in the hominy and cook for about 1 hour.
16. Serve with the remaining onion, cilantro and lime juice.

Azteca
Tacos

🥣 Prep Time: 15 mins
🕐 Total Time: 25 mins

Servings per Recipe: 9
Calories	379 kcal
Fat	21.4 g
Carbohydrates	28.1g
Protein	20.3 g
Cholesterol	58 mg
Sodium	69 mg

Ingredients

2 lb. top sirloin steak, cut into thin strips
salt and ground black pepper to taste
1/4 C. vegetable oil
18 (6 inch) corn tortillas
1 onion, diced

4 fresh jalapeno peppers, seeded and chopped
1 bunch fresh cilantro, chopped
4 limes, cut into wedges

Directions

1. Heat a large skillet on medium-high heat and cook the steak for about 5 minutes.
2. Season with the salt and pepper and transfer into a plate and keep warm.
3. In the same skillet, heat the oil.
4. Place 1 tortilla in the hot oil and cook till browned lightly, turning once.
5. Repeat with the remaining tortillas.
6. Place the tortillas on a plate and top each one with the steak, onion, jalapeño and cilantro.
7. Drizzle with the lime juice.

CINNAMON STICKS
from Mexico
(Churros)

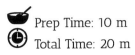

Prep Time: 10 m
Total Time: 20 m

Servings per Recipe: 4
Calories	691 kcal
Fat	51.1 g
Carbohydrates	57.1g
Protein	3.3 g
Cholesterol	0 mg
Sodium	293 mg

Ingredients
1 C. water
2 1/2 tbsp white sugar
1/2 tsp salt
2 tbsp vegetable oil
1 C. all-purpose flour

2 quarts oil for frying
1/2 C. white sugar, or to taste
1 tsp ground cinnamon

Directions
1. In a small pan, mix together the water, 2 1/2 tbsp of the sugar, salt and 2 tbsp of the vegetable oil on medium heat and bring to a boil.
2. Remove from the heat and add the flour and mix till a ball forms.
3. In a deep skillet, heat the oil to 375 degrees F.
4. With a pastry bag, pipe the strips of the dough in the hot oil and fry till golden.
5. Drain onto a paper towel.
6. In a shallow dish, mix together 1/2 C. of the sugar and cinnamon.
7. Roll the drained churros in the sugar mixture.

How to Make
Chimichangas

Prep Time: 20 mins
Total Time: 45 mins

Servings per Recipe: 6
Calories	1595 kcal
Fat	83.7 g
Carbohydrates	1133.4g
Protein	79.8 g
Cholesterol	1215 mg
Sodium	2322 mg

Ingredients
1 1/2 C. chicken broth
1 C. uncooked long-grain rice
1/2 C. red enchilada sauce
1 1/2 onion, diced, divided
6 (12 inch) flour tortillas
4 C. diced cooked chicken breast, divided
1 lb. Monterey Jack cheese, shredded, divided
1 (6 oz.) can sliced black olives
4 C. refried beans, divided
1/4 C. vegetable oil

Topping
3 avocados, peeled and pitted
1/2 C. finely chopped cilantro
2 tbsp lemon juice
3 green onions, diced
1/4 C. finely chopped jalapeno chili peppers
1 tomato, diced
2 C. shredded lettuce
1 C. sour cream
2 C. shredded Cheddar cheese

Directions
1. In a medium pan, mix together the broth, rice, sauce and 1 diced onion and bring to a boil.
2. Reduce the heat to low and simmer for about 20 minutes.
3. Meanwhile, heat tortillas in a large skillet till soft enough to fold.
4. Place the chicken onto each tortilla, followed by the shredded Jack cheese, diced onion, olives, rice mixture and beans.
5. Roll the tortillas, tucking in sides to secure the filling.
6. In a large skillet, heat the oil and fry the filled tortillas, till browned from all sides.
7. Drain on paper towels.
8. In a medium bowl add the avocados, cilantro, lemon juice, green onions, chili peppers and tomatoes and mash to combine.
9. In a platter, place the shredded lettuce and top with the chimichangas, avocado mixture, sour cream and shredded Cheddar cheese.

TAMPICO
Inspired Meal Pie

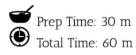

Prep Time: 30 m
Total Time: 60 m

Servings per Recipe: 16
Calories	432 kcal
Fat	23.9 g
Carbohydrates	33.3g
Protein	19.8 g
Cholesterol	68 mg
Sodium	847 mg

Ingredients

2 lb. ground beef
1 onion, chopped
2 tsp minced garlic
1 (2 oz.) can black olives, sliced
1 (4 oz.) can diced green chili peppers
1 (10 oz.) can diced tomatoes with green chili peppers
1 (16 oz.) jar taco sauce

2 (16 oz.) cans refried beans
12 (8 inch) flour tortillas
9 oz. shredded Colby cheese

Directions

1. Set your oven to 350 degrees F before doing anything else.
2. Heat a large skillet on medium heat and cook the beef for about 5 minutes.
3. Add the onion and garlic, and sauté for about 5 minutes.
4. Drain any excess fat.
5. Stir in the olives, green chili peppers, tomatoes with green chili peppers, taco sauce and refried beans and reduce the heat to low.
6. Simmer for about 15-20 minutes.
7. In the bottom of a large casserole dish, place a thin layer of the beef mixture.
8. Top with a layer of the tortillas, followed by the beef mixture and a layer of the cheese.
9. Repeat the layers till all the ingredients are used.
10. Cook in the oven for about 20-30 minutes.

Lumberjack
Fajitas

Prep Time: 25 mins
Total Time: 2 h 50 mins

Servings per Recipe: 6

Calories	357 kcal
Fat	29.2 g
Carbohydrates	4.6g
Protein	14.1 g
Cholesterol	39 mg
Sodium	235 mg

Ingredients

1 1/2 lb. beef round steak
1/4 C. tequila
1/2 C. fresh lime juice
1/2 C. cooking oil
2 tbsp liquid smoke
1 tsp Worcestershire sauce

1/4 tsp ground black pepper
1/2 tsp salt
3/4 tsp paprika
1/2 C. sliced onion
3/4 C. bell peppers, sliced into thin strips

Directions

1. In a plastic bag, mix together the steak, tequila and lime juice and refrigerate to marinate for about 2 hours.
2. Set your outdoor grill for high heat and lightly grease the grill grate.
3. Remove the steak from the bag and discard the marinade.
4. Cook the steak on grill for about 8 minutes per side.
5. Remove the steak from the grill and slice into 1/4-inch strips.
6. In a serving plate, arrange the strips.
7. In a skillet, heat the oil on medium heat.
8. Stir in the liquid smoke, Worcestershire sauce, pepper, salt and paprika to the oil and heat the mixture.
9. Add the onions and peppers and cook till the peppers become tender.
10. Place the mixture over the steak strips and serve immediately.

NACHOS
Jamaican Style

 Prep Time: 30 m
Total Time: 40 m

Servings per Recipe: 4
Calories	336.7
Fat	20.7g
Cholesterol	103.5mg
Sodium	787.1mg
Carbohydrates	10.6g
Protein	28.8g

Ingredients
jamaican jerk spice
1 red bell pepper, seeded and chopped finely
1 yellow bell pepper, seeded and chopped finely
2 boneless skinless chicken breasts, boiled

and chopped
1 lemon
1 (12 1/2 oz.) bags taco flavor Doritos
2 C. four-cheese Mexican blend cheese

Directions
1. Set your oven to 400 degrees F before doing anything else.
2. Coat the chicken with about 3 tbsp of the jerk spice.
3. In a bowl, mix together the bell peppers and lemon juice.
4. In the bottom of a large baking dish, place 1 bag of the Doritos, followed by the chicken and cheese.
5. Cook everything in the oven till the cheese is melted.
6. Just before serving, add the bell peppers and mix.

A South
American Salad

🥣 Prep Time: 5 mins
🕐 Total Time: 25 mins

Servings per Recipe: 8
Calories   100 kcal
Fat   4.4 g
Carbohydrates   15.1g
Protein   2 g
Cholesterol   0 mg
Sodium   195 mg

Ingredients

1 (8 oz.) package yellow rice mix
1 1/4 C. water
2 tbsp olive oil
1 (15 oz.) can black beans, rinsed and drained
1 (15.25 oz.) can whole kernel corn, drained
2 tsp lime juice
1 tsp ground cumin

Directions

1. In a pan, mix together the rice, water and olive oil on high heat and bring to a boil.
2. Reduce the heat to medium-low and simmer, covered for about 20-25 minutes.
3. In a large bowl, mix together the beans, corn, lime juice and cumin.
4. Stir in the cooked rice and serve.

SWEET
Paprika Nachos

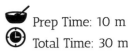

Prep Time: 10 m
Total Time: 30 m

Servings per Recipe: 4
Calories	634.3
Fat	39.4g
Cholesterol	95.6mg
Sodium	1031.3mg
Carbohydrates	40.9g
Protein	30.4g

Ingredients
1/2 lb. ground beef
1 tsp chili powder (Mexican blend)
1/2 tsp salt
1/2 tsp dried onion flakes
1/8 tsp sweet paprika
2 tbsp water
8 restaurant-style corn tortilla chips
1/2 C. refried beans

1 1/2 C. shredded cheddar cheese
1/2 C. shredded monterey jack cheese
1/4 C. diced onion
1 large jalapeno pepper

Directions
1. Set your oven to 375 degrees F before doing anything else.
2. Heat a large skillet and cook the beef until it is browned completely.
3. Drain the fat from the skillet.
4. Add the dried onion, paprika, chili powder, salt and water and reduce the heat to low.
5. Simmer for about 10 minutes.
6. In a pan, add the beans and cook till heated through.
7. In a small bowl, mix together the both cheeses.
8. In a large pie plate, place the tortilla chips.
9. Place about 1 tbsp of the beans over each chip, followed by about 2 tbsp of the beef mixture, cheese mixture, onion and 1 slice of jalapeño pepper.
10. Cook everything in the oven for about 8-10 minutes.

Cream Cheese
and Corn Casserole

Prep Time: 15 mins
Total Time: 60 mins

Servings per Recipe: 8
Calories	265 kcal
Fat	22.1 g
Carbohydrates	14.8g
Protein	4.8 g
Cholesterol	63 mg
Sodium	173 mg

Ingredients

1 (8 oz.) package cream cheese
1/2 C. butter
1/2 C. milk
1 (16 oz.) package frozen corn

1 red bell pepper, diced
8 fresh jalapeno peppers, diced

Directions

1. Set your oven to 350 degrees F before doing anything else.
2. In a pan, melt the cream cheese and butter on medium-low heat.
3. Add the milk and mix till smooth and bubbly.
4. In a medium casserole dish, mix together the frozen corn, red bell pepper and jalapeño peppers.
5. Add the cream cheese mixture and toss to coat.
6. Cook in the oven for about 35-45 minutes.

EAST LA
Style Nachos

Prep Time: 15 m
Total Time: 60 m

Servings per Recipe: 4
Calories	222.6
Fat	9.1g
Cholesterol	37.7mg
Sodium	85.0mg
Carbohydrates	23.1g
Protein	15.6g

Ingredients
2 boneless skinless chicken breasts, cut into small strips.
1/2 C. lime juice
1 tsp pepper
1 tsp chili powder
2 tbsp olive oil
1 C. frozen corn kernels

1/3 C. red onion, chopped
1 tbsp lime juice
1 tsp cumin
tortilla chips

Directions
1. In a bowl, mix together the chicken, olive oil, 1/4 C. of the lime juice, chili powder and black pepper and refrigerate to marinate for about 30 minutes.
2. Meanwhile, cook the corn till desired doneness.
3. In a bowl, add the onion, corn and the remaining lime juice and toss to coat.
4. Heat a large nonstick frying pan and cook the chicken till the desired doneness.
5. Transfer the chicken into the bowl, with the corn mixture and mix well.
6. Top the tortilla chips with the chicken mixture and serve.

Santa Clara
Pudding

Prep Time: 20 mins
Total Time: 1 h 20 mins

Servings per Recipe: 8
Calories	174 kcal
Fat	7.3 g
Carbohydrates	26.7g
Protein	2.4 g
Cholesterol	1 mg
Sodium	271 mg

Ingredients

5 tbsp margarine, softened
1/4 C. masa harina
1/3 C. white sugar
1/2 C. water
2 C. frozen whole-kernel corn, thawed

1/2 C. cornmeal
1 tsp baking powder
1/2 tsp salt
4 tsp milk

Directions

1. In a medium bowl, add the margarine, masa flour and sugar and mix light and fluffy.
2. In a food processor, add 1 C. of the corn kernels, water and cornmeal and pulse till just smooth.
3. Add the corn mixture into the masa mixture and mix well.
4. Add the remaining corn, baking powder, salt and milk and mix till smooth.
5. Transfer the mixture into a double boiler over a large pan of the simmering water.
6. With a foil paper, cover the pan tightly and steam for about 50-60 minutes.
7. Stir the pudding before serving to give it a consistent texture.

MEXICO CITY
Fajitas

🍳 Prep Time: 10 m
🕐 Total Time: 35 m

Servings per Recipe: 8	
Calories	397 kcal
Fat	16.6 g
Carbohydrates	19.9 g
Protein	40.3 g
Cholesterol	104 mg
Sodium	821 mg

Ingredients

3 tbsp vegetable oil
6 (6 oz.) skinless, boneless chicken breast halves, thinly sliced
1/2 C. sliced onions
1/2 C. sliced red bell pepper
1/2 C. tomato juice

2 tbsp taco seasoning mix
1 C. salsa
8 (1/2 inch thick) slices French bread
2 C. shredded Cheddar cheese

Directions

1. In a large skillet, heat the oil on medium-high heat and cook the chicken for about 5 minutes.
2. Stir in the sliced onions and red peppers and cook for about 5 minutes.
3. Stir in the tomato juice and taco seasoning and cook for about 7 minutes.
4. Set the broiler of your oven and arrange oven rack about 6-inches from the heating element.
5. Spread 2 tbsp of salsa over each slice of French bread and top with the chicken mixture evenly.
6. Sprinkle each sandwich with 1/4 C. of the Cheddar cheese.
7. Cook the sandwiches under the broiler for about 5 minutes.

Spicy Honey
Tilapia Tacos

🥣 Prep Time: 35 mins
🕐 Total Time: 6 h 44 mins

Servings per Recipe: 6
Calories	416 kcal
Fat	19.2 g
Carbohydrates	38.5g
Protein	22.6 g
Cholesterol	43 mg
Sodium	644 mg

Ingredients

Marinade
1/4 C. extra virgin olive oil
2 tbsp distilled white vinegar
2 tbsp fresh lime juice
2 tsp lime zest
1 1/2 tsp honey
2 cloves garlic, minced
1/2 tsp cumin
1/2 tsp chili powder
1 tsp seafood seasoning
1/2 tsp ground black pepper
1 tsp hot pepper sauce
1 lb. tilapia fillets, cut into chunks
Dressing

1 (8 oz.) container light sour cream
1/2 C. adobo sauce from chipotle peppers
2 tbsp fresh lime juice
2 tsp lime zest
1/4 tsp cumin
1/4 tsp chili powder
1/2 tsp seafood seasoning
salt and pepper to taste
Toppings
1 (10 oz.) package tortillas
3 ripe tomatoes, seeded and diced
1 bunch cilantro, chopped
1 small head cabbage, cored and shredded
2 limes, cut in wedges

Directions

1. For marinade in a bowl, add the olive oil, vinegar, lime juice, lime zest, honey, garlic, cumin, chili powder, seafood seasoning, black pepper and hot sauce and beat till well combined.
2. In a shallow dish, add the tilapia and marinade and mix. Refrigerate, covered for about 6 - 8 hours.
3. For the dressing in a bowl, mix together the sour cream and adobo sauce..
4. Stir in the lime juice, lime zest, cumin, chili powder, seafood seasoning, salt and pepper.
5. Refrigerate, covered till serving.
6. Set your outdoor grill for high heat and lightly, grease the grill grate.
7. Arrange the grill grate 4 - inch from the heat.
8. Remove the tilapia from marinade and discard off any excess marinade.
9. Cook the tilapia on the grill for about 9 minutes, flipping once in the middle way.
10. For the tacos, place the tilapia pieces in the center of each tortilla with the desired amounts of tomatoes, cilantro, and cabbage.
11. Top with the dressing.
12. Roll up the tortillas around the fillings and serve with a garnishing of the lime wedges.

MEXICAN
Macho Bake

Prep Time: 15 m
Total Time: 35 m

Servings per Recipe: 6
Calories   740.0
Fat   54.5g
Cholesterol   151.8mg
Sodium   501.3mg
Carbohydrates   27.0g
Protein   35.7g

Ingredients
1 1/2 lb. ground beef, cooked
1/2 can refried beans
16 oz. sour cream

8 oz. shredded cheddar cheese
1 bag tortilla chips, crushed

Directions
1. Set your oven to 350 degrees F before doing anything else.
2. In a bowl, mix together the beans and beef.
3. Transfer the beef mixture into a casserole dish, followed by the sour cream, cheese.
4. With foil, cover the casserole dish and cook everything in the oven for about 15-20 minutes.
5. Uncover and top everything with the crushed tortilla chips.
6. Cook everything in the oven for about 5 minutes.

Mexican
Skillet

Prep Time: 20 mins
Total Time: 30 mins

Servings per Recipe: 4
Calories	212 kcal
Fat	4.6 g
Carbohydrates	36.8g
Protein	10.1 g
Cholesterol	0 mg
Sodium	818 mg

Ingredients

1 tbsp olive oil
1 large onion, chopped
3 cloves garlic, minced
4 small zucchini, diced
1 fresh poblano chili pepper, seeded and chopped
1 C. frozen whole kernel corn
1 (15 oz.) can black beans, rinsed and drained
1/2 tsp salt

Directions

1. In a large skillet, heat the oil on medium-high heat and sauté the onion and garlic till tender.
2. Add the zucchini and poblano pepper, and sauté till soft.
3. Stir in the corn and beans and cook till heated completely.
4. Season with the salt to taste

LATIN
COUSCOUS

🍲 Prep Time: 15 m
🕐 Total Time: 25 m

Servings per Recipe: 4
Calories	300 kcal
Fat	10.9 g
Cholesterol	44.8g
Sodium	7.1 g
Carbohydrates	0 mg
Protein	713 mg

Ingredients
1 C. couscous
1/2 tsp ground cumin
1 tsp salt
1 1/4 C. boiling water
1 clove unpeeled garlic
1 (15 oz.) can black beans, rinsed and drained

1 C. canned whole kernel corn, drained
1/2 C. finely chopped red onion
1/4 C. chopped fresh cilantro
1 jalapeno pepper, minced
3 tbsp olive oil
3 tbsp fresh lime juice

Directions
1. In a large bowl, mix together the couscous, cumin and salt.
2. Add the boiling water and stir to combine.
3. Tightly, cover with a plastic wrap and keep aside for about 10 minutes.
4. Meanwhile in a small skillet, cook the unpeeled garlic clove on medium-high heat till toasted and the skin has turned golden-brown.
5. Peel the garlic clove and mince it.
6. Add the minced garlic, the black beans, corn, onion, cilantro, jalapeño pepper, olive oil and lime juice in the bowl with couscous and mix.
7. Serve warm or cold as well.

Mexi-Mesa
Casserole

🥄 Prep Time: 20 mins
🕐 Total Time: 60 mins

Servings per Recipe: 4
Calories   703 kcal
Fat   40.2 g
Carbohydrates   75.8g
Protein   14.7 g
Cholesterol   36 mg
Sodium   246 mg

Ingredients

4 (8 oz.) yams
1 medium red bell pepper, seeded and diced
2 avocados - peeled, pitted, and mashed
1/4 C. chopped fresh cilantro
1/4 C. olive oil

2 green onions, sliced
1/2 tsp ground cumin
3 tbsp lime juice
salt and ground black pepper to taste
1 C. shredded Cheddar cheese

Directions

1. Set your oven to 350 degrees F before doing anything else.
2. Arrange the yams onto a baking sheet and cook in the oven for about 40 minutes, flipping occasionally.
3. In a bowl, mix together the red pepper, avocado, cilantro, olive oil, green onions, cumin and lime juice.
4. Remove the yams from the oven and cut in half lengthwise, then with a fork, fluff the centers.
5. Top with the avocado stuffing and sprinkle with the salt and pepper.
6. Serve with a sprinkling of the shredded Cheddar cheese.

ENCHILADA
and Nachos

Prep Time: 5 m
Total Time: 10 m

Servings per Recipe: 6
Calories	672.6
Fat	34.0g
Cholesterol	48.7mg
Sodium	973.7mg
Carbohydrates	75.2g
Protein	20.1g

Ingredients
1 C. enchilada sauce
1 lb. tortilla chips
2 (16 oz.) cans refried beans, heated

1 -2 C. shredded cheddar cheese
1 C. sour cream

Directions
1. Divide the tortilla chips in serving plates.
2. Serve with the remaining ingredients as nachos.

Catalina's
Secret Fajitas

Prep Time: 10 mins
Total Time: 60 mins

Servings per Recipe: 12

Calories	112 kcal
Fat	7.2 g
Carbohydrates	4.3g
Protein	7.3 g
Cholesterol	18 mg
Sodium	20 mg

Ingredients

1/4 C. lime juice
1/4 C. chopped fresh cilantro
1/2 jalapeno pepper, seeded and minced
2 tbsp olive oil
2 cloves garlic, minced
1 tsp ground cumin

1 1/2 lb. beef skirt steak, cut across the grain into 1/2-inch strips
1 yellow onion, cut into 1/2-inch strips
3 red bell peppers, cut into 1/2-inch strips
2 tsp vegetable oil, divided

Directions

1. In a large glass bowl, add the lime juice, cilantro, jalapeño pepper, olive oil, garlic and cumin and beat well.
2. Add the skirt steak, onion and red bell peppers and toss to coat evenly.
3. With a plastic wrap, cover the bowl and marinate to refrigerator for about 30 minutes to 2 hours.
4. Remove the steak, onion, and peppers from marinade and shake off the excess.
5. Discard remaining marinade.
6. In a large skillet, heat 1 tsp of the vegetable oil on high heat and sear the steak for about 3 minutes per side.
7. Transfer the steak into a plate and cover with a foil paper for about 5 minutes.
8. In the same skillet, heat the remaining oil on medium-high heat and sauté the onion and peppers for about 5-6 minutes.
9. Stir in the steak and cook till heated completely.

MANDARIN
Margaritas

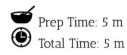 Prep Time: 5 m

Total Time: 5 m

Servings per Recipe: 2
Calories	180 kcal
Carbohydrates	20.5 g
Cholesterol	0 mg
Fat	0.2 g
Protein	0.6 g
Sodium	5 mg

Ingredients

1 cup fresh tangerine juice
1 cup ice
2 (1.5 fluid oz.) premium tequila blanco
1 tbsp agave nectar

Directions

1. Blend all the ingredients mentioned above until the required smoothness is achieved.
2. Serve.

Palo
Pepperjack Potatoes

Prep Time: 20 mins

Total Time: 1 h 30 mins

Servings per Recipe: 6

Calories	625 kcal
Fat	24.3 g
Carbohydrates	89.8g
Protein	16.9 g
Cholesterol	48 mg
Sodium	1023 mg

Ingredients

6 large baking potatoes
3 tbsp olive oil
3/4 C. sour cream
1 1/2 C. shredded pepperjack cheese
2 (11 oz.) cans Mexican-style corn,
drained
2 (4 oz.) cans chopped green chili peppers,
drained

Directions

1. Set your oven to 400 degrees F before doing anything else.
2. With a fork, pierce each potato several times and rub with the oil generously.
3. Arrange the potatoes onto a baking sheet and cook in the oven for about 45-55 minutes.
4. Meanwhile, in a bowl, add the sour cream, cheese, corn and chilis and mix.
5. Remove the potatoes from the oven and keep aside to cool slightly.
6. Cut a slit in the top of the each potato and scoop out the flesh, leaving about 1/2-inch thick shell.
7. Add the potato flesh in the bowl with the cheese mixture and mix well.
8. Fill the potato shells with the potato mixture evenly.
9. Arrange the potatoes on a baking sheet and cook in the oven for about 15 minutes.

FATHIA'S
Fajitas

Prep Time: 30 m

Total Time: 50 m

Servings per Recipe: 4

Calories	257 kcal
Fat	12.6 g
Carbohydrates	19.7g
Protein	17.4 g
Cholesterol	49 mg
Sodium	136 mg

Ingredients
2 skinless, boneless chicken breast halves, cut into 1/4-inch wide strips
1 lime, juiced
1/2 tsp ground cumin
1/4 tsp paprika
1/4 tsp chili powder
1/8 tsp cayenne pepper
1/8 tsp ground black pepper
1 tbsp olive oil

1 red bell pepper, cut into 1/4 inch strips
1/2 large red onion, sliced 1/4-inch thick
4 (6 inch) corn tortillas
1/4 C. sour cream, divided
1/2 C. shredded Cheddar-Monterey Jack cheese blend, divided
1 C. shredded lettuce, divided
1/2 C. diced tomato, divided

Directions
1. In a large bowl, mix together the chicken strips, lime juice, cumin, paprika, chili powder, cayenne pepper and black pepper.
2. Marinate the chicken for about 15-30 minutes.
3. In a large skillet, heat the oil on medium heat and sauté the red bell pepper and onion for about 5 minutes.
4. Move the vegetables to the sides of the skillet.
5. Place chicken strips with marinade in the center of the skillet and cook for about 3 minutes.
6. Stir the chicken with the vegetables and cook for about 2 minutes.
7. Remove from the heat and keep aside.
8. In a microwave-safe plate, place the corn tortillas with damp paper towels separating each tortilla and microwave for about 30 seconds.
9. Arrange the corn tortillas onto 4 serving plates and spread 1 tbsp of the sour cream over each tortilla.
10. Top each tortilla with 1/4 of the chicken mixture, followed by 2 tbsp of the shredded Cheddar-Monterey Jack cheese blend, 1/4 C. of the lettuce and 2 tbsp of the diced tomato.
11. Repeat with the remaining tortillas and ingredients.
12. Top with the desired toppings and serve.

Rice
with Spice

Prep Time: 25 mins
Total Time: 35 mins

Servings per Recipe: 2
Calories 590 kcal
Fat 26.9 g
Carbohydrates 68.5g
Protein 23.2 g
Cholesterol 50 mg
Sodium 692 mg

Ingredients

1 tbsp vegetable oil
1 onion, chopped
1 tsp minced garlic
1 1/2 C. vegetable broth
1 1/2 C. instant brown rice
2 tsp chili powder

1 jalapeno pepper, seeded and minced
1/2 tsp ground cumin
1 red bell pepper, chopped
1 large tomato, seeded and chopped
1 C. shredded Monterey Jack cheese

Directions

1. In a large pan, heat the oil on medium high heat and sauté the onion and garlic for about 3 minutes.
2. Stir in the broth, rice, chili powder, jalapeño peppers and cumin and bring to a boil on high heat.
3. Reduce the heat and simmer, covered for about 4 minutes.
4. Stir in the bell pepper and simmer, covered for about 5 minutes.
5. Stir in the tomato and shredded cheese into hot cooked rice.

ZUCCHINI
Dreaming

🥣 Prep Time: 20 m
🕐 Total Time: 50 m

Servings per Recipe: 6
Calories	121 kcal
Fat	4.9 g
Carbohydrates	17.8g
Protein	4.8 g
Cholesterol	6 mg
Sodium	83 mg

Ingredients
2 1/2 C. fresh corn kernels
1 tbsp olive oil
1/4 C. chopped onion
1 clove garlic, minced
1 lb. zucchini, sliced
3 roma (plum) tomatoes, chopped
1 fresh poblano chili pepper - seeded,
deveined, and chopped
salt and black pepper to taste
1/4 C. crumbled cotija cheese

Directions
1. In a pan, add the corn and enough water to cover and bring to a boil.
2. Reduce the heat to medium and cook, covered for about 10 minutes.
3. Then drain well.
4. In a large skillet, heat the oil on medium-high heat and sauté the onion and garlic for about 5 minutes.
5. Add the zucchini and tomato and cook for about 5 minutes.
6. Stir in the corn kernels, poblano pepper, salt and pepper and cook, covered for about 10 minutes.
7. Serve with a sprinkling of the cotija cheese.

Taco
Seasoning I

🍲 Prep Time: 1 mins
🕐 Total Time: 1 mins

Servings per Recipe: 1 oz.
Calories	5 kcal
Carbohydrates	0.9 g
Cholesterol	0 mg
Fat	0.2 g
Protein	0.2 g
Sodium	185 mg

Ingredients

1 tbsp chili powder
1/4 tsp garlic powder
1/4 tsp onion powder
1/4 tsp crushed red pepper flakes
1/4 tsp dried oregano

1/2 tsp paprika
1 1/2 tsps ground cumin
1 tsp sea salt
1 tsp black pepper

Directions

1. Take out all the ingredients mentioned above and combine them thoroughly.
2. Store in an airtight container.
3. Use for aforementioned recipes.
4. Enjoy.

REFRIED
Beans

Prep Time: 15 m
Total Time: 8 h 15 m

Servings per Recipe: 15
Calories	139 kcal
Carbohydrates	25.4 g
Cholesterol	0 mg
Fat	0.5 g
Protein	8.5 g
Sodium	785 mg

Ingredients
1 onion, peeled and cut in half
3 cups dry pinto beans, rinsed
1/2 fresh jalapeno pepper, seeded and chopped
2 tbsps minced garlic
5 tsps salt

1 3/4 tsps fresh ground black pepper
1/8 tsp ground cumin, optional
9 cups water

Directions
1. Cook onion, jalapeno, garlic, rinsed beans, salt, pepper, and cumin after adding water on high heat in a slow cooker for about 8 hours.
2. Now take out the beans and mash them with a potato masher before putting them into the liquid again and heating it again to get the required consistency.

Thursday's
Stovetop Fajitas

Prep Time: 10 mins
Total Time: 20 mins

Servings per Recipe: 4

Calories	518 kcal
Fat	14.1 g
Carbohydrates	60.1g
Protein	34.1 g
Cholesterol	69 mg
Sodium	1117 mg

Ingredients

1 tbsp vegetable oil
1 lb. boneless, skinless chicken breasts, thinly sliced
1 (14 oz.) bag Birds Eye(R) Recipe Ready Tri-Color Pepper & Onion Blend
1 tsp ground cumin or fajita seasoning

blend
1 tsp salt
8 flour tortillas, warmed

Directions

1. In a large nonstick skillet, heat oil on medium-high heat and cook the chicken for about 5 minutes, stirring occasionally.
2. Stir in the Recipe Ready Tri-Color Peppers & Onions Blend, cumin and salt and cook for about 5 minutes, stirring occasionally.
3. Serve in the flour tortillas and serve with a garnishing of the lime wedges.

MEXICAN
Rice

Prep Time: 5 m
Total Time: 30 m

Servings per Recipe: 5

Calories	158 kcal
Carbohydrates	29.1 g
Cholesterol	1 mg
Fat	2.8 g
Protein	3.4 g
Sodium	631 mg

Ingredients

1 cup long grain white rice
1 tbsp vegetable oil
1 1/2 cups chicken broth
1/2 onion, finely chopped
1/2 green bell pepper, finely chopped
1 fresh jalapeno pepper, chopped
1 tomato, seeded and chopped

1 cube chicken bouillon
salt and pepper to taste
1/2 tsp ground cumin
1/2 cup chopped fresh cilantro
1 clove garlic, cut in half

Directions

1. Cook rice in hot oil for about 3 minutes on medium heat in a pan before adding chicken broth and bringing it to a boil.

2. Now add onion, diced tomato, green pepper, jalapeno, bouillon cube, salt and pepper, cumin, cilantro, and garlic.

3. Bring this mixture to a boil and turn the heat down to low, and cook for another 20 minutes.

4. Serve.

Taco
Seasoning II

Prep Time: 5 mins
Total Time: 5 mins

Servings per Recipe: 3 tbsps	
Calories	21 kcal
Carbohydrates	4.6 g
Cholesterol	0 mg
Fat	0.4 g
Protein	0.4 g
Sodium	596 mg

Ingredients

1 tbsp cornstarch
2 tsps chili powder
1 tsp salt
1 tsp paprika
1 tsp white sugar

1/2 tsp onion powder
1/2 tsp garlic powder
1/4 tsp cayenne pepper
1/2 tsp ground cumin

Directions

1. Combine all the spices together in a bowl and store it in an airtight container.
2. Use for any meat which you desire to have a Mexican style taste or for meat to be placed on the grill.
3. Enjoy.

ELOTE
(Corn on the Cob Mexican Street Food)

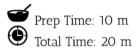

Prep Time: 10 m
Total Time: 20 m

Servings per Recipe: 4
Calories   386 kcal
Carbohydrates   28.9 g
Cholesterol   53 mg
Fat   29.1 g
Protein   8.4 g
Sodium   368 mg

Ingredients

4 ears corn, shucked
1/4 cup melted butter
1/4 cup mayonnaise

1/2 cup grated cotija cheese
4 wedges lime (optional)

Directions

1. First, preheat your grill for medium heat before starting anything else.
2. Now take out the corn and grill it on the preheated grill for about 10 minutes or until lightly brown.
3. Cook it in some melted butter and evenly spread mayonnaise over it.
4. Also add some cojita cheese before serving for extra flavor.
5. Enjoy.

NOTE: Grilled corn with mayo and cheese is very addicting.

Tex-Mex
Nachos

Prep Time: 10 mins
Total Time: 20 mins

Servings per Recipe: 2
Calories   162.8
Fat   5.7g
Cholesterol   3.1mg
Sodium   267.7mg
Carbohydrates   22.5g
Protein   7.8g

Ingredients

1 whole wheat pita bread, cut each half into 8 triangles
1/4 avocado
1 tomatoes

30 g low-fat cheese
ground black pepper
1/4 C. coriander

Directions

1. Set your oven to 355 degrees F before doing anything else.
2. In 2 large baking sheets, place the pita triangles in a single layer and cook everything in the oven for about 5 minutes.
3. In a bowl, mix together the tomato, avocado, 1 tbsp of the cheese, salt and black pepper.
4. In 2 small baking dishes, divide the tomato mixture evenly.
5. Divide the pita triangles between both dishes and gently, push in the tomato mixture, then sprinkle with the remaining cheese.
6. Cook everything in the oven for about 5 minutes.
7. Serve with a garnishing of the cilantro.

AGUA FRESCA
(Mexican Watermelon Based Drink)

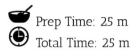

Prep Time: 25 m
Total Time: 25 m

Servings per Recipe: 8
Calories	72 kcal
Carbohydrates	18.7 g
Cholesterol	0 mg
Fat	0.1 g
Protein	0.5 g
Sodium	2 mg

Ingredients
4 cups cubed seeded watermelon
1/2 cup water
1/2 cup white sugar, or to taste

4 slices lime
24 fresh mint leaves
ice

Directions
1. Add watermelon and some water into the blender and blend it until smooth before adding the sugar.
2. Now cut lime slices in half and place each half in every glass along with mint leaves.
3. Now fill each glass with ice cubes and pour in the blended watermelon.
4. Stir it a bit before serving.
5. Enjoy.

Horchata I
(Classical Spanish Milk Based Drink)

🥣 Prep Time: 10 mins
🕐 Total Time: 3 h 10 mins

Servings per Recipe: 10
Calories	213 kcal
Carbohydrates	48.4 g
Cholesterol	2 mg
Fat	0.6 g
Protein	2.9 g
Sodium	16 mg

Ingredients
1 cup uncooked white long-grain rice
5 cups water
1/2 cup milk
1/2 tbsp vanilla extract

1/2 tbsp ground cinnamon
2/3 cup white sugar

Directions
1. Blend rice and water in a food processor for about 1 minute and let it stand as it is for about three hours.
2. Now take out all the water from it and in this water add milk, sugar, cinnamon and vanilla.
3. Mix well and serve it in a glass over ice.

NOTE: This is a classical form of horchata other forms can be made with almonds, or barley, see next recipe for a tasty variation.

HORCHATA II
(Coconut Based)

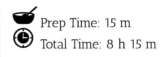 Prep Time: 15 m

Total Time: 8 h 15 m

Servings per Recipe: 15

Calories	322 kcal
Carbohydrates	36.5 g
Cholesterol	11 mg
Fat	17.6 g
Protein	7.1 g
Sodium	72 mg

Ingredients
1 cup uncooked white rice
1 cup almonds
1 cup sweetened flaked coconut
3 cups boiling water
1 (14 oz.) can coconut milk

1 (14 oz.) can sweetened condensed milk
5 cups cold water, or more as needed
5 cups ice

Directions
1. Blend rice, coconut flakes and almonds in a blender until really fine.
2. Pour boiling water into this mixture and let it stand for at least 6 hours.
3. Now take remove the water and add sweetened condensed milk and coconut milk to it.
4. Pour this over ice cubes in a glass.
5. Enjoy.

Mexican-Style
Hot Chocolate

Prep Time: 10 mins
Total Time: 15 mins

Servings per Recipe: 12

Calories	118 kcal
Carbohydrates	16.1 g
Cholesterol	12 mg
Fat	4.2 g
Fiber	0.7 g
Protein	4.4 g
Sodium	99 mg

Ingredients

1 1/2 cups cold water
1/2 cup white sugar
1/4 cup unsweetened cocoa powder
2 tbsps all-purpose flour
1 tsp ground cinnamon
1/4 tsp ground cloves

1/4 tsp salt
6 cups whole milk
1 tbsp vanilla extract

Directions

1. Mix cold water, cocoa powder, sugar, flour, cinnamon, cloves, and salt in a pan very thoroughly before putting it over low heat and cooking it for about 4 minutes.
2. Now add milk and cook for another two minutes before adding vanilla extract.
3. Blend this in a food processor until the required smoothness is achieved.

MARIA'S FAVORITE DRINK
(Honeydew Juice)

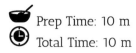

Prep Time: 10 m
Total Time: 10 m

Servings per Recipe: 6
Calories	159 kcal
Carbohydrates	40.3 g
Cholesterol	0 mg
Fat	0.5 g
Fiber	3 g
Protein	2 g
Sodium	71 mg

Ingredients
1 (5 pound) honeydew melon, quartered and seeded
2 cups ice cubes
1 cup water

3 tbsps white sugar

Directions
1. Remove the flesh from the honeydew melon quarters and place into the blender along with ice cubes, sugar and water.
2. Blend this until you see that the sugar has dissolved.
3. Enjoy.

Restaurant Style
Stir Fry

Prep Time: 10 mins
Total Time: 25 mins

Servings per Recipe: 4

Calories	98.1
Fat	7.2g
Cholesterol	0.0mg
Sodium	5.4mg
Carbohydrates	8.1g
Protein	1.1g

Ingredients

1 lb boneless lean beef (top round, sirloin)
2 garlic cloves, minced
1 large red bell pepper, cut into strips
1 large onion, thinly sliced and separated
3 tbsp lime juice
2 tbsp oil
2 tsp cumin
1/2 tsp cornstarch

flour tortilla
avocado
tomatoes
salsa
sour cream
cheese

Directions

1. Cut the beef into 1-inch long and 1/8-inch strips
2. In a skillet, heat 1 tbsp of the oil on high heat and stir fry the beef strips for about 1 1/2-2 minutes.
3. Transfer the beef strips into a bowl.
4. In the same skillet, heat 1 tbsp of the oil and sauté the garlic, onion and green pepper for about 3 minutes.
5. Meanwhile in a bowl, mix together the cumin, lime juice and cornstarch.
6. Add the cornstarch mixture into the skillet and stir to combine.
7. Add the beef strips and stir fry till the mixture is hot and bubbly.
8. Transfer the mixture into a bowl.
9. Serve in tortillas with the desired garnishing.

CELEBRATION MEXICAN
Fajita Marinade

Prep Time: 15 m
Total Time: 1 d 15 m

Servings per Recipe: 8
Calories	457 kcal
Fat	11.2 g
Carbohydrates	77.4g
Protein	20.5 g
Cholesterol	2 mg
Sodium	1678 mg

Ingredients
3 limes, juiced
2 green onions, chopped
3 cloves garlic, minced
3 tbsp chopped fresh cilantro
2 tbsp vegetable oil

1/2 tsp red pepper flakes
1/4 tsp ground coriander
1/4 tsp ground anise seed (optional)

Directions
1. In a bowl, add all the ingredients and mix till well combined.
2. Pour mixture over your favorite meat.
3. Refrigerate, covered to marinate for about 12-24 hours before cooking as desired.

Zucchini
Fajita Bake

🥄 Prep Time: 30 mins
🕐 Total Time: 1 h 25 mins

Servings per Recipe: 8
Calories	457 kcal
Fat	11.2 g
Carbohydrates	77.4g
Protein	20.5 g
Cholesterol	2 mg
Sodium	1678 mg

Ingredients

1/2 zucchini, cut into 1/4-inch slices
1 C. red bell pepper slices
1 onion, cut into 1/4-inch slices and separated into rings
1 C. water
1 tsp vegetable oil
1 (1.27 oz.) packet dry fajita seasoning
1/2 C. all-purpose flour
1/2 C. nutritional yeast
1 tsp salt
1 1/2 tsp garlic powder
1/2 tsp dry mustard powder
2 C. water
1/4 C. margarine

2 (10 oz.) cans red enchilada sauce
5 (9 inch) whole-wheat tortillas, torn into 1-inch pieces
1 1/2 C. cooked brown rice
3 (15 oz.) cans black beans, rinsed and drained
1 tbsp sliced black olives (optional)
1/4 avocado - peeled, pitted and diced (optional)
2 tbsp chopped tomato (optional)
1 jalapeno pepper, seeded and thinly sliced (optional)
2 tbsp chopped onion (optional)
2 tbsp prepared salsa (optional)
2 tbsp sour cream (optional)

Directions

1. Set your oven to 350 degrees F before doing anything else.
2. In a large bowl, mix together the zucchini, red bell pepper, and 1 onion, 1 C. of the water, vegetable oil and dry fajita seasoning.
3. Marinate for about 1-2 hours then drain the vegetables.
4. Heat a large skillet on medium heat and cook the vegetables for about 10 minutes.
5. Transfer the vegetables into a bowl and keep aside.
6. In a pan, place the flour, nutritional yeast, salt, garlic powder, dry mustard powder and 2 C. of the water and beat till well combined.
7. Place the pan on medium heat and bring to a boil.
8. Reduce the heat to low and simmer for about 5 minutes, beating continuously.

9. Stir in the margarine and remove from the heat.

10. Spread 1/2 can of enchilada sauce in the bottom of a 13x9-inch baking dish evenly.

11. Top with 1/4 of the tortilla pieces, followed by 1/2 C. of the brown rice.

12. Place 1/3 of the cooked vegetables over the brown rice.

13. Spread 1 can of the black beans over the vegetables and top with 1/4 of the nutritional yeast sauce evenly.

14. Repeat the layers twice.

15. Make a final layer with the remaining 1/4 of the tortilla pieces, remaining nutritional yeast sauce and remaining 1/2 can of the enchilada sauce.

16. Cook in the oven for about 30-45 minutes.

17. Remove from the oven and keep aside for about 10 minutes.

18. Top the casserole with the black olives, avocado, tomato, jalapeno pepper, 2 tbsp of chopped onion, salsa and sour cream before serving.

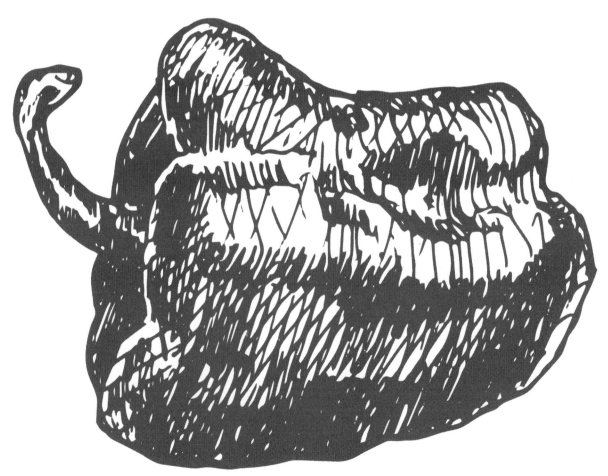

Orange
Chili Beef

🥣 Prep Time: 30 mins
🕐 Total Time: 10 h 50 mins

Servings per Recipe: 4	
Calories	234 kcal
Fat	10.7 g
Carbohydrates	16.9g
Protein	19.4 g
Cholesterol	31 mg
Sodium	1070 mg

Ingredients
1 flank steak
1/4 C. shichimi togarashi (optional)
1/4 C. orange juice
1/4 C. low-soy sauce
2 tbsp lime juice
1/2 orange, zested
1/2 lime, zested
1 tbsp cornstarch
1 tbsp chili powder, or more to taste
1 tsp kosher salt
1 tsp smoked paprika

1 tsp brown sugar
1 tsp cayenne pepper
1 tsp red pepper flakes
1/2 tsp onion powder
1/2 tsp garlic powder
1/2 tsp ground cumin
1 tbsp olive oil
1 onion, cut into slices and separated
1 red bell pepper, cut into thin strips
3/4 C. water

Directions
1. With a meat mallet, flatten the flank steak slightly and rub the shichimi togarashi on both sides of the steak.
2. In a plastic wrap, wrap the steak and refrigerate for 8 hours or overnight.
3. In a resealable plastic bag, mix together the orange juice, soy sauce, lime juice, orange zest, and lime zest.
4. Remove the flank steak from plastic wrap and place in the resealable plastic bag to coat with the marinade.
5. Squeeze out the excess air and seal the bag.
6. Refrigerate to marinate for about 2 hours.
7. Set your outdoor grill for high heat and grease the grill grate.
8. Remove the steak from the marinade and preserve the marinade into a small bowl.
9. Cook steak on the grill for about 8-10 minutes per side, basting with the marinade after every 5 minutes.

10. Cut the steak in half lengthwise and then cut across the grain into thin slices.

11. In a bowl, add the cornstarch, chili powder, salt, paprika, brown sugar, cayenne pepper, red pepper flakes, onion powder, garlic powder and ground cumin and beat till well combined.

12. In a large skillet, heat the oil on medium-high heat and sauté the onion and red bell pepper for about 5-10 minutes.

13. Add the sliced steak, chili powder mixture and water and cook for about 3-5 minutes.

Picnic
Nachos

Prep Time: 15 mins
Total Time: 30 mins

Servings per Recipe: 4
Calories   1612.3
Fat   129.7g
Cholesterol   405.8mg
Sodium   4498.4mg
Carbohydrates   21.8g
Protein   88.6g

Ingredients

white corn tortilla chips
1 lb. zesty hot sausage
1 lb. ground beef
2 (4 oz.) cans mild green chilies
1 (1 1/4 oz.) packets taco seasoning
2 C. salsa

1 bunch green onion, chopped
4 C. shredded Mexican blend cheese
8 oz. sour cream
aluminum foil
cooking spray

Directions

1. Cut a sheet of foil into 4 sheets to make packets that will cover the tortilla chips with toppings.
2. Grease each foil sheet with the cooking spray.
3. Divide the nacho chips in the middle of each foil sheet.
4. Place your desired toppings over the nacho chips.
5. Fold the foil around the filling to make packets.
6. Place the packets onto a grill over a low burning campfire.
7. Cook over the campfire for about 10-15 minutes.
8. Serve with a topping of sour cream.

MAYAN
Mocha Powder

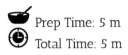 Prep Time: 5 m

Total Time: 5 m

Servings per Recipe: 12
Calories	122 kcal
Carbohydrates	28.2 g
Cholesterol	1 mg
Fat	0.4 g
Fiber	0.8 g
Protein	3.1 g
Sodium	37 mg

Ingredients

2/3 cup nonfat dry milk powder
2/3 cup instant coffee granules
1 1/3 cups white sugar
1/3 cup unsweetened cocoa powder
1 1/2 tsps pumpkin pie spice

1/2 tsp ground cinnamon
1/4 tsp ground red pepper

Directions

1. Combine all ingredients mentioned above and put them in an airtight container.
2. Serve.

Atole
(Spanish Hot Corn Drink)

Prep Time: 5 mins
Total Time: 15 mins

Servings per Recipe: 5

Calories	68 kcal
Carbohydrates	14.1 g
Cholesterol	0 mg
Fat	0.4 g
Fiber	2.3 g
Protein	1.1 g
Sodium	8 mg

Ingredients
1/2 cup masa (corn flour)
5 cups water
1 tbsp ground cinnamon
5 tbsps piloncillo, brown sugar cones

1 tbsp vanilla extract

Directions
1. Blend masa, piloncillo, water and cinnamon in a food processor for about 3 minutes or until smooth
2. Now bring this mixture to a boil over medium heat before turning down the heat to low and cooking for another five minutes.
3. Remove this saucepan from heat and add vanilla.
4. Pour this into mugs and serve hot.

CLASSICAL
Sangrita

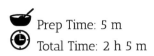 Prep Time: 5 m
Total Time: 2 h 5 m

Servings per Recipe: 5
Calories	33 kcal
Carbohydrates	8.1 g
Cholesterol	0 mg
Fat	0.1 g
Fiber	0.2 g
Protein	0.5 g
Sodium	105 mg

Ingredients
1/4 cup fresh lime juice
1 paper-thin onion slice
1 cup fresh orange juice
1 dash Mexican-style hot sauce (such as
Valentina or Cholula), or to taste
salt to taste

Directions
1. Mix onion slice and lime juice in a medium sized bowl and let it stand as it is for about 3 hours.
2. Remove onion from the juice and add salt, orange juice and hot sauce.
3. Serve it cold.

Mexican
Style Ceviche

Prep Time: 40 mins
Total Time: 40 mins

Servings per Recipe: 8

Calories	62 kcal
Carbohydrates	9.3 g
Cholesterol	6 mg
Fat	2 g
Fiber	1.6 g
Protein	2.9 g
Sodium	241 mg

Ingredients

1 (8 oz.) package imitation crabmeat, flaked
2 large tomatoes, chopped
1 red onion, finely chopped
1/2 bunch cilantro, chopped

2 limes, juiced
3 serrano peppers, finely chopped
1 tbsp olive oil
salt and pepper to taste

Directions

1. Put shredded imitation crab in a glass bowl and mix olive oil thoroughly before adding serrano peppers, cilantro, tomato and onion.
2. Pour some lime juice over the contents and add some salt and pepper according to your taste.
3. Allow it to cool down for one hour before serving.

FAJITA
Casserole

Prep Time: 20 m
Total Time: 50 m

Servings per Recipe: 8
Calories	411.7
Fat	12.7g
Cholesterol	64.7mg
Sodium	118.1mg
Carbohydrates	45.0g
Protein	27.5g

Ingredients

1 1/2 lbs lean ground beef
2 garlic cloves, minced
1 green bell pepper, coarsely chopped
1 red bell pepper, coarsely chopped
1 lb elbow macaroni
1/2 C. sliced green onion, divided
1 tsp ground cumin

1/8-1/4 tsp cayenne pepper
2 (15 1/2 oz.) jars salsa con queso
1 C. crushed tortilla chips, divided
3/4 C. shredded colby-monterey jack cheese
1 tsp chopped cilantro

Directions

1. Set your oven to 350 degrees F before doing anything else and lightly, grease a 13x9-inch baking dish.
2. Heat a large skillet and cook the beef, peppers and garlic till browned completely.
3. Drain the grease from the skillet.
4. Meanwhile cook the macaroni according to package's directions.
5. Drain well.
6. Add the cooked macaroni into the beef mixture with 1/4 C. of the green onions, seasonings, salsa con queso and 1/2 C. of the crushed chips and mix.
7. Transfer the beef mixture into the prepared baking dish.
8. Top with the remaining 1/2 C. of the crushed tortilla chips and remaining 1/4 C. of the green onions.
9. Sprinkle with the cheese and cilantro evenly.
10. Cook in the oven for about 30 minutes.

Ameri-Mex
Nachos

Prep Time: 5 mins
Total Time: 5 mins

Servings per Recipe: 4

Calories	381.0
Fat	22.9g
Cholesterol	123.5mg
Sodium	1001.3mg
Carbohydrates	7.9g
Protein	34.4g

Ingredients

1 lb. extra lean ground beef
7 C. tortilla chips
1/2 lb. Velveeta cheese, pasteurized prepared cheese product cut into 1/2-inch cubes

1 C. shredded lettuce
1/2 C. chopped tomato
1/4 C. sliced black olives
1/3 C. sour cream

Directions

1. Heat a large skillet and cook the beef till cooked completely done, and drain the fat completely.
2. In a large microwave safe platter, place the tortilla chips and top everything with the Velveeta cheese and microwave on high for about 2 minutes.
3. In a bowl, mix together the beef and remaining ingredients.
4. Place the beef mixture over the chips and serve.

MEXICAN GREEN
Papaya Salad

Prep Time: 20 m
Total Time: 50 m

Servings per Recipe: 6
Calories	168 kcal
Carbohydrates	26.9 g
Cholesterol	0 mg
Fat	5.1 g
Fiber	7.9 g
Protein	6.4 g
Sodium	313 mg

Ingredients
Dressing:
1/4 cup chopped fresh cilantro, or to taste
3 cloves garlic, minced, or more to taste
2 limes, juiced
2 tbsps olive oil
1 tbsp brown sugar
1 pinch chili powder, or more to taste
(optional)
salt to taste

Salad:
1 green papaya, peeled and shredded
2 cups cold cooked black beans
1 cup cold cooked corn
1 red bell pepper, cut into small dice

Directions
1. Blend cilantro, garlic, olive oil, brown sugar, lime juice, chili powder and salt in a blender until the right consistency is achieved.
2. Add this to a mixture of corn, papaya, red bell pepper and black beans in a large sized bowl.
3. Serve.

Enchilada
Sauce

Prep Time: 20 mins
Total Time: 50 mins

Servings per Recipe: 12

Calories	43 kcal
Carbohydrates	6.1 g
Cholesterol	0 mg
Fat	2.2 g
Fiber	1.7 g
Protein	1 g
Sodium	35 mg

Ingredients
1 tbsp vegetable oil
1 cup diced onion
3 tbsps chopped garlic
1 tsp dried oregano
1 tsp ground cumin
1/4 tsp ground cinnamon

3 tbsps all-purpose flour
5 tbsps hot chili powder
4 1/2 cups chicken broth
1/2 (1 oz.) square semi-sweet chocolate
(optional)

Directions
1. Cook onion in hot oil over medium heat in a pan until tender and add garlic, cinnamon, oregano and cumin, and cook for another two minutes.
2. Now add flour and chili powder, and let the sauce get thick.
3. Now add chicken broth and cook until the sauce has reached a thick state again.
4. Combine chocolate and let it melt.
5. Serve.

MEXICAN DESSERT
Mango Nachos

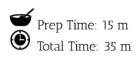 Prep Time: 15 m

Total Time: 35 m

Servings per Recipe: 4	
Calories	752.9
Fat	30.3g
Cholesterol	81.9mg
Sodium	837.7mg
Carbohydrates	112.9g
Protein	10.8g

Ingredients

Cinnamon Cream
1 C. whipping cream
2 -3 tbsp sugar
1/8 tsp cinnamon
Nachos
6 fajita-size flour tortillas, cut each into 6 wedges

oil (for frying)
1/4 C. sugar
1 tsp cinnamon
1/2 C. caramel sauce
1 1/2 C. diced mangoes

Directions

1. For the cinnamon cream, in a bowl, add all the ingredients and beat till stiff peaks form.
2. Transfer the cream into a serving bowl and refrigerate.
3. For the nachos, in a skillet, heat the oil and fry the wedges in batches till golden brown.
4. With a slotted spoon, transfer everything onto a paper towel lined plate to drain.
5. In a bowl, mix together the cinnamon and sugar.
6. Add fried wedges and toss to coat well and arrange into a serving platter.
7. In a microwave safe bowl, place the caramel sauce and microwave on high for about 20 - 30 seconds.
8. Pour the sauce over the wedges and top with the chopped mango.
9. Serve with a topping of cinnamon cream.

Nachos Mex-Mediterranean

Prep Time: 10 mins
Total Time: 10 mins

Servings per Recipe: 6
Calories	156.8
Fat	9.3g
Cholesterol	17.8mg
Sodium	342.3mg
Carbohydrates	14.6g
Protein	4.6g

Ingredients

2 tbsp finely chopped kalamata olives
2 tbsp finely chopped sun-dried tomatoes packed in oil (from 7 oz. jar)
2 tsp oil from jar sun-dried tomatoes
1 small plum tomato, finely chopped and drained

1 medium green onion, thinly sliced (1 T)
4 oz. restaurant-style corn tortilla chips
1 (4 oz.) packages feta cheese, finely crumbled

Directions

1. In a bowl, mix together all the ingredients except the tortilla chips and cheese.
2. In a microwave safe platter, place the tortilla chips in a single layer and top them with the cheese and microwave everything on high for about 1 minute.
3. Rotate the plate and continue microwaving for about 30-60 seconds more.
4. Top everything with the vegetables mixture and serve.

SOUTHWEST
Neufchatel
Nacho Soup

 Prep Time: 5 m

Total Time: 30 m

Servings per Recipe: 8
Calories	330.5
Fat	21.3g
Cholesterol	107.0mg
Sodium	1484.3mg
Carbohydrates	3.9g
Protein	29.4g

Ingredients
Soup
2 lb. lean ground beef
salt (or to taste)
1/2 tsp pepper
4 C. beef broth
10 oz. diced tomatoes and green chilies
6 oz. neufchatel cheese, cut into cubes

6 oz. Velveeta cheese, cut into cubes
Garnish
shredded cheese
sour cream
hot sauce

Directions
1. Heat a large soup pan and cook the beef until it is browned completely.
2. Drain the fat from the skillet and stir in the salt and black pepper.
3. Add the tomatoes and broth and bring everything to a boil.
4. Simmer, covered for about 15 minutes.
5. Stir in the Velveeta cheese and cream cheese and cook on medium - low heat till the cheese melts.
6. Serve with a topping of sour cream, shredded cheese and hot sauce.

Copy-Cat
Fajitas

Prep Time: 15 mins

Total Time: 55 mins

Servings per Recipe: 6

Calories	395 kcal
Fat	12.9 g
Carbohydrates	49.5g
Protein	22.3 g
Cholesterol	45 mg
Sodium	1234 mg

Ingredients

4 boneless, skinless chicken breast halves
1 tbsp ground cinnamon
salt and pepper to taste
2 large baking potatoes, peeled and cubed
1/4 C. canola oil
1 large yellow onion, chopped

1 large clove garlic, peeled and minced
1 tbsp chopped jalapeno peppers
1 lime, juiced
12 (6 inch) corn tortillas, warmed

Directions

1. Set your oven to 400 degrees F before doing anything else.
2. In a shallow baking dish, place the potatoes.
3. Drizzle with about 1/2 of the oil and sprinkle with the salt evenly.
4. Cook in the oven for about 30-40 minutes.
5. Meanwhile season the chicken with the cinnamon, salt and pepper.
6. In another baking dish, place the chicken breast halves and cook in the oven for about 30 minutes.
7. Remove from the oven and let it cool.
8. After cooling, shred the chicken breast halves.
9. In a skillet, heat the remaining oil on medium heat and sauté the onion and garlic till tender.
10. Stir in the shredded chicken, jalapeño and lime juice and cook till heated completely.
11. Serve the chicken and potatoes in warmed tortillas.

FAJITA-ITOS
from Cali

Prep Time: 4 m
Total Time: 10 m

Servings per Recipe: 4
Calories	355 kcal
Fat	18.6 g
Carbohydrates	43.4g
Protein	17.4 g
Cholesterol	30 mg
Sodium	456 mg

Ingredients
4 Mission(R) Soft Taco Flour Tortillas
2 cloves garlic, minced
1/2 jalapeno pepper, minced
1/2 tsp ground cumin
1/4 C. cilantro, chopped
2 limes, juiced
1 tsp sugar
2 tbsp olive oil
1 (12 oz.) flank steak

1/2 C. tomatoes, cut into large chunks
1 tbsp crumbled cotija cheese
4 Bibb lettuce leaves
Salt and pepper as needed
1 C. frozen sweet corn kernels
1/2 C. red onion, diced
1 Poblano pepper, cut into strips

Directions
1. In a bowl, add the garlic, jalapeño, cumin, cilantro, lime juice, sugar and oil and beat till well combined.
2. Transfer the marinade into a plastic gallon-size zip top bag.
3. Add the flank steak and refrigerate to marinate for about 1-4 hours.
4. In a platter, assemble the tomatoes, cheese and lettuce leaves.
5. Set your grill for medium-high heat and arrange an 8-inch cast iron pan directly on the grill.
6. Remove the steak from the marinade, and pat dry with the paper towel.
7. Season with the salt and pepper.
8. Cook the steak on grill for about 6-8 minutes per side.
9. Remove from the grill and keep aside for about 5 minutes before slicing into 1/2-inch thick slices.
10. Meanwhile, grease a preheated cast iron pan with non-stick spray.
11. Add the corn, red onion and Poblano peppers and sauté for about 6-8 minutes.
12. At the same time, coat the tortillas with non-stick spray.
13. Cook the tortillas on grill for about 30 seconds from both sides.
14. Immediately place the sliced steak on top of the corn mixture in cast iron pan and serve sizzling hot.